The Prayer of Fire

The Prayer of Fire
Experiencing the Lord's Prayer

Lorraine Kisly

Foreword by Philip Zaleski

PARACLETE PRESS
BREWSTER, MASSACHUSETTS

Library of Congress Cataloging-in-Publication Data

Kisly, Lorraine.
The prayer of fire : experiencing the Lord's prayer / Lorraine Kisly.
  p. cm.
Includes bibliographical references.
ISBN 1-55725-359-5 (pbk.)
1. Lord's prayer. I. Title.
BV230.K49 2004
226.9'606–dc22   2004002074

10 9 8 7 6 5 4 3 2 1

Published by Paraclete Press
Brewster, Massachusetts
www.paracletepress.com

Printed in the United States of America.

Prayer will become for you rather a state than a precise and deliberate act.

Abbé Huvelin to Baron von Hügel, 1886

Table of Contents

Foreword

In the late summer of 1941, the French intellectual, essayist, and mystic Simone Weil (1909–1943) entered for the first time in her brief life the endless green garden of prayer. Until then, by her own admission, she had never addressed God silently or in words, had never participated in liturgical prayer, had never encountered those childhood devotions so familiar to millions of French boys and girls. Weil's great awakening began when she took up, in the course of acquiring modern Greek, the Lord's Prayer—or as she invariably called it, the "Our Father." She memorized the prayer (in Greek) and recited it daily upon arising and while at work in the annual vineyard harvest. The effect was electrifying. Sometimes the first words would catapult her to "a place outside space," where she discovered "infinity to the second or sometimes the third degree," a mysterious realm filled with silence, which Weil describes not as a lack of sound but as a "positive sensation"—the presence, she seems to suggest, of the unconditionally Real. Sometimes, in the midst of this fertile silence, Christ would appear, as if called forth by her prayer, and he would "take possession" of her with incomparable clarity and majesty.

Weil's experience with the Lord's Prayer, for all its remarkable fireworks, is best read as a sustained moment of epiphany in the often humdrum, lifelong process of *metanoia*, a critical stage in a work of spiritual rebirth that began for her at the age of fourteen, when she set herself the task of attaining what she called "the kingdom of truth," and that ended twenty years later when she died of starvation and exhaustion among the workers of Occupied France. That is to say, in a sense there is nothing exceptional about Weil's experience with the Lord's Prayer. Accidentals (Greek language, French landscape) aside, what happened to Weil may happen to anyone who recites the prayer with comparable attention and love as part of a life devoted to spiritual renewal. Or it may be, on the other hand, that someone may say the prayer for years or a lifetime with no discernible mystical experience. The work of the prayer may be invisible, unfolding only in the most secret chambers of the soul. What remains constant, whether or not mystical graces descend, is the prayer's inexhaustible power, for to recite it is to place oneself in the presence of God, to open oneself to supernatural help, to undertake what St. Paul calls putting on "the new man . . . created in righteousness and holiness." The Lord's Prayer is the monarch of prayers, summation of the Gospels, essence of faith; to receive its gifts, one need only approach it with open mind, clean heart, and good will. That God will respond is certain; it is no accident that Jesus, immediately following the description of the prayer in Luke's Gospel, assures us "Ask, and it will be given you;

search, and you will find; knock and the door will be opened to you" (Luke 11:9).

But therein lies the difficulty: How to invite the Lord's Prayer into one's life? How to approach it as Jesus intended? How to voice it with open mind, clean heart, and good will? Answering these questions is not an optional matter; the Lord's Prayer is, as Lorraine Kisly says, "a revelation, a present word," and it is incumbent upon each of us, as creatures born of flesh and of spirit, to listen to this word as best we can.

This is the great gift of the book that you hold in your hands. Many other volumes on the Lord's Prayer address theological, literary, and historical matters. Lorraine Kisly points us in a different direction: she helps us to hear the prayer anew, to stand humbly before its mysteries, to explore how its every petition and declaration might reverberate within our being, how to begin to answer its call so that it may bear fruit, so that Christ may descend and "take possession" of us. This is a book on prayer that rings with the spirit of prayer. It teems with practical advice, on matters as varied as finding a good place to pray, the cultivation of attention, and postures that help deepen the experience of prayer. But more important than all this counsel is Kisly's ceaseless emphasis upon listening, upon learning to be watchful, to be awake, to remain alert for God's still, small voice, to surrender with humility and thanks to the grace and love of our Lord as transmitted through his prayer.

A book like this must be read with care. It deals in weighty matters and delivers its ideas with subtlety of mind and simplicity of spirit. I think it will help immeasurably to place yourself in a quiet, receptive frame of mind before you begin the first chapter. Remember who you are, remember to whom you pray. Put aside the chirping cleverness that so often accompanies your reading. Read slowly and reflectively. Once you have finished the book, you will have time to digest and, if you wish, to question what you have read.

To help in this digestion, you may want to explore further in the history and meaning of the Lord's Prayer. By all means, study the scriptural accounts in Luke and Matthew; learn how the prayer has inspired two thousand years of Church history, influencing saints and martyrs, philosophers and popes; pore over the four great traditional treatises on the prayer by Sts. Augustine, Cyprian, John Chrysostom, and Cyril; ponder how the prayer—addressed to the Father, revealed by the Son, filled with the Holy Spirit— expresses the self-reflective love of the Trinity; above all, strive ceaselessly to conform your own life to that of the prayer, for as St. Cyprian writes, "nor was it only in words, but in deeds also, that the Lord taught us to pray." These historical, theological, scriptural, and moral explorations will deepen your prayer, and they will, most certainly, lead you back to the foundational experience of listening that lies at the heart of Kisly's admirable book. Describing this act of listening, Kisly quotes Dietrich Bonhoeffer to the effect that "the words which come from God will be the steps upon which we find our way to God." The Lord's Prayer is the quintessential staircase to God, and all time spent upon its steps—even clinging helplessly to its balustrade—bears fruit, for to listen attentively to even one of its divine phrases is to participate, however imperfectly, in the life of God, to begin to heed his word, to embrace his will, and mirror his love.

Philip Zaleski

Editor of the *Best American Spiritual Writing* series.
Other books include *The Recollected Heart* and *The Book of Heaven* (with Carol Zaleski).

Introduction

This is a book for beginners. It is for those who sense that in the Lord's Prayer is found the heart of the Christian Way, and who wish through their own experience and their own understanding to enter into this living heart. It is for readers who, while still beginners, know enough to know that this work cannot be done for them, and who are ready to commit themselves to a discipline and a practice.

To listen to the Lord's Prayer is to follow a practice that relates us directly to Christ as Teacher, as Master. The prayer he teaches us is a revelation, a present word; and this book is in the spirit of listening to this word and opening to this revelation. Theological, literary, linguistic, hermeneutical, and many other valuable forms of argument and analysis of the prayer must be sought elsewhere.

The book uses the Revised Standard Version of the prayer as found in Matthew. There is some agreement among scholars that the shorter version in Luke was recorded earlier, but that the longer version of the prayer in Matthew is closer to the original as given by Jesus. The doxology, "For thine is the kingdom, and the power, and the glory now and forever, Amen," has been added nearly from the outset. It is an altogether fitting close to the prayer, but because Jesus did not speak it, it is not included here.

The prayer Jesus gave to us is complete, peerless, and indestructible. Everything said about it is by comparison babble and prating, and the only value of such words is to direct us again and again to the most sacred and most holy word of the Lord. May an ever-deepening encounter with the Lord's Prayer accomplish in us what Christ intends.

L. K.

The Lord's Prayer

Our Father who art in heaven,
Hallowed be thy name.
Thy kingdom come,
Thy will be done,
On earth as it is in heaven.
Give us this day our daily bread;
And forgive us our debts,
As we also have forgiven our debtors;
And lead us not into temptation,
But deliver us from evil.

CHAPTER 1

The Epiphany of the Lord's Prayer

This prayer, the Our Father, contains the fullness of perfection. It was the Lord Himself who gave it to us as both an example and a rule. It raises up those making use of it . . . to that prayer of fire known to so few. It lifts them up, rather, to that ineffable prayer which rises above all human consciousness, with no voice sounding, no tongue moving, no words uttered. The soul lights up with heavenly illumination and no longer employs constricted, human speech. All sensibility is gathered together and, as though from some very abundant source, the soul breaks forth richly, bursts out unspeakably to God, and in the tiniest instant it pours out so much more than the soul can either describe or remember when it returns again to itself.

John Cassian (360–435)

From the earliest days of Christianity the primacy of the prayer given to us by Christ has been recognized by church fathers, theologians, saints, and laymen. Throughout the last two thousand years, the Lord's Prayer has been at the center of every form and rule of prayer among Christians, and it remains so to this day. But so many of us *recite* the prayer. We say it as we have said it since earliest childhood. We have all heard it countless times, but when have we last listened to it?

To listen to the Lord's Prayer is to begin a journey to the heart of the Christian promise of deep and intimate relationship with God. Turning toward the words of the Lord's Prayer again, this time with body, mind, heart, and spirit, to listen (as did those first listeners) rather than to *say* it, we will discover the Our Father as the primary Christian meditation. Through the practice of intensely alert and attentive listening, we will witness in silent communion the unfolding of each compressed and generative phrase. The prayer will indeed raise us to that "ineffable prayer which rises above all human consciousness, with no voice sounding, no tongue moving, no words uttered."

The sayings and parables of Christ are inexhaustible, new at each true encounter, and so too is each word of the prayer he taught us. The Lord's Prayer is an organic whole, a living word of God whose depths can never be known completely. "As with the Gospels," writes Orthodox priest Alexander Schmemann, "the Lord's Prayer is always addressed to each of us personally anew, in a way which makes it seem to have been composed specifically for me, for my needs, for my questions, for my pilgrimage. Yet, at the same time it remains eternal and unchanging in its essence, always calling us to what is most important, to the ultimate, to the highest."

We are not often able to perceive the spiritual realities that lie behind each phrase of the prayer. It is toward these unknown depths that we will try to find our way as we begin our journey.

PRAYING IN THE NOW

Let's first understand what the prayer is not. It is not a creed, not a composition or a compilation, not an example of Christian prayer, but the fountain from which all Christian prayer flows. It is not something we all recite together and *believe*, but a revelation from a divine source that will never stop calling to us. A sublime and numinous teaching, it bids us enter the kingdom at this very moment. It is not revelation in the sense of an historical event, but a revelation that we can receive now and that is always new.

Gregory of Nyssa wrote that in the Lord's Prayer, Christ

> does not hide the supernal glory in darkness, making it difficult for those who want to contemplate it; but He first illumines the darkness by the brilliant light of His teaching and then grants the pure of heart the vision of the ineffable glory in shining splendor. The water He gives us for sprinkling does not come from alien streams, but wells up in ourselves, whether we understand by it the fountains of tears

streaming from our eyes, or the pure conscience of the heart that admits no impurity coming from evil.

. . .

For this is the force of His words, that we should learn by them not to pronounce certain sounds and syllables, but the meaning of the ascent to God which is accomplished through a sublime way of life.

Gregory tells us that the water of life given to us by Christ comes not "from alien streams" but wells up within us. The prayer, listened to with a quiet presence and collected attention, reminds us of who we are and where we belong. We recognize and remember our spiritual home and come to know "the meaning of the ascent to God."

It is necessary to understand more about each phrase of the prayer, certainly, and we need to ponder its meaning. But this is not our task at the time of prayer. When we pray, we must learn to allow the prayer to act upon us. For this, time and our attention are required: we will need patience with ourselves and fidelity to our practice. Simone Weil wrote that under these conditions the Lord's Prayer is capable of transforming our being: "The Our Father is to prayer what Christ is to humanity. It is impossible to say it once through, giving the fullest possible attention to each word, without a change, infinitesimal perhaps but real, taking place in the soul." Day by day, week by week, the prayer brings us into a different world. Our self-love is challenged, the shell of our egotism is cracked, the presence of others made more real. Every living, breathing creature, all organic life, the earth and all creation begin to reveal their sanctity. Praise flickers unbidden. We begin to sense that we are being worked upon. Dwelling within the Lord's Prayer a channel for grace is opened, and grace begins to flow.

Our attention makes possible the exchange between what is above and what is below, and brings us into relationship. But to give our full attention does not mean to clamp our minds down upon a single thought so that distractions are held forcibly at bay. We are to open our hands, not clench our fists. To enter into the radiance of the Lord's Prayer is to move from reciting the prayer to listening, to becoming what one theologian calls "essential hearers." When we attend to the prayer, phrase by phrase, in silence, we are brought into a divine atmosphere. The kingdom begins to appear, here and now. Another level comes into view.

"The Our Father is a Eucharist," Roman Catholic Louis Evely writes, "a placing of ourselves absolutely at God's disposal, an absolute restitution, an absolute opening of our arms, an absolute assent, an absolute agreement. At that precise moment, we are no longer of this world. . . . We have passed for the space of a prayer, into his own." It is this movement into a reality usually closed to us that is offered in the prayer, a movement requiring all our desire, all our attention, all our care. We turn aside from our preoccupations, our demands, our aims and ends and means, and turn instead to a Presence waiting for us in the silence.

The prayer is a teacher, and with its help we can be led into this living relationship. Bishop Seraphim Sigrist says of the prayer that it is "intermediate between the divine world and the human world, linking the two in one breathing out, and breathing in, and in one circulation."

The whole of the prayer relates the human and divine in the present moment, a present that includes "now and ever, and unto the ages of ages." Each petition of the prayer orients us towards this eternal now. While each phrase is indeed a petition, it is not a petition in the sense of a request to be granted in the future. The prayer reveals all as the will of God, and asks us to apprehend and to be aligned with what this divine will intends. This becomes clearer when we reaffirm the petitions, recognizing the ever-present work of God:

> Our Father who art in heaven—
> *may we know thy love*
> Hallowed be Thy name—
> *may we see thy glory*
> Thy kingdom come—
> *may we enter it*
> Thy will be done on earth as it is in heaven—
> *may we obey it*
> Give us this day our daily bread—
> *may we take and eat with thanksgiving*
> And forgive us our debts as we also have
> forgiven our debtors—
> *may we receive thy mercy as we forgive others*

And lead us not into temptation—
may we forsake ourselves and seek you
But deliver us from evil—
*may our trust in you keep us from the way of
death and grant us life.*
Amen.

This reading wis one of the many thousands possible—the prayer resists being pinned down once and for all. Each phrase moves between two poles, evoking a whole that can never be finally encompassed. We pray for the coming of the kingdom, and yet are told it has already come and is nearer to us than hands and feet. We pray that the will of God be done, but could it ever be thwarted? And so on through the prayer: we beg forgiveness and yet *are* forgiven. Clinging to one meaning or another, the analytical part of the mind is ever confounded. This quality of yes/and—of yes and *another* yes—along with the prayer's simplicity and brevity, has ensured that it has come down to us without distortion. Its memorable phrases of great power defy both reduction and explanation and after two thousand years of human history the prayer is as pure and as fresh as the moment it was uttered. This incorruptibility must surely have been intentional and is one of its remarkable qualities.

The Lord's Prayer is a doorway leading to remembrance at every moment and in every circumstance of life. Johannes Kelpius, an early American mystic, spoke of the need for such constant remembrance in what he called "inward prayer," a prayer of the heart that is performed at all times and places, a prayer that never ceases. To make a beginning toward this, he directs us to the Lord's Prayer.

> O whoever you are that have not a constant custom and promptitude to perform this inward prayer! You know the Lord's Prayer, in which you have enough to perform this inward prayer, although you knew nothing else. Every petition of it contains so much that one may perform a good long ardent contemplation on it. But when these petitions are repeated, and we penetrate into them livingly or ruminate on them in our hearts, it has a quite different effect than when they are uttered with the mouth only. Experience will teach it you.

It is this experience we need. Nothing will allow us to approach the promise of the Lord's Prayer but our own experience of it. Let us begin.

CHAPTER 2

Becoming Attuned

Begin as you are and where you are, with your own history and your own understanding. The experience of others won't help you unless it resonates with what is already within you. The alchemist's dictum that in order to make gold one must have some gold of one's own, and Christ's teaching that to him who has, more shall be given both point to this truth.

Repeat the Lord's Prayer slowly, once through. Pause between each phrase or between several words as seems appropriate to you.

Do you remember saying each word of the prayer? Were you attracted to certain passages? Did you react negatively to others? Did you say the words of the prayer but lack a sense of praying? Short as the prayer is, were you nonetheless distracted and unable to give it your attention from beginning to end? Where did the words resonate? Did they begin and end in the mind only? Were you aware of your body and your breathing?

Do you have expectations when you say the prayer? Do you know what they are? Are you disappointed in either the prayer or yourself, feeling somehow you have failed or the prayer has failed you?

Or instead is the prayer familiar and reassuring? Does it have comforting childhood associations? Does it make you feel that everything is all right, that you belong, and that nothing bad can happen to you?

Are you afraid that the meaning of the Lord's Prayer eludes you? Do you want to "get" something from the prayer? What is it?

To deepen our encounter with the Lord's Prayer, we have to know for ourselves where we stand. Each time we say the prayer we embark on a journey into the unknown. We are unknown to ourselves, and the meaning of the prayer is only partially perceived at each approach. Familiarity with the taste of my habitual self and with the words of the prayer does nothing to alter this essential truth. For most of us, each time we begin, God is a concept, the prayer itself is an idea, and I myself am not present. I may not feel like praying. My mind may be filled with distractions that at that moment are not so much distractions as the center of my interest.

There is no sense in denying reality. The only possible starting point is wherever we are, with our experience of the moment. To be sincere while praying we must heed Christ's word: knowing us, and knowing our need, he urges us not only to pray but to watch. This is not a command or an injunction. It is a counsel, full of understanding, full of kindness and compassion for our situation, full of love and care. Watch and pray, he tells us. He knows us, and he knows our condition: we are situated in freedom and yet subject to many forces both within and without. "Because he himself was tested by what he suffered, he is able to help those who are being tested" (Hebrews 2:18). He knows our nature, our weakness, and our yearning. He has already fully anticipated every contradiction and difficulty we may encounter.

"WHERE ARE YOU?" ↗

To watch means to be awake, to be sober, to be aware and mindful. It also can have the connotation of being on guard. Watching and praying, we are in the present moment, at the source of the impulses alive within us, whether we approve of them or not, whether we judge them a hindrance or a help. As we watch in an attitude of prayer, in an attitude of confidence and dependence, then indirectly—but very certainly—the Lord's Prayer awakens the divine gift of conscience within us. In the light of conscience we are granted the ability to see whether the impulses flowing within us are leading us toward relationship or toward a narrow self-sufficiency. Not merely an ethical compass, the voice within that discerns right from wrong, conscience is self-knowledge under the gaze of God, an inner searching that asks "Where are you?" An organ of perception, conscience is the intelligence of the heart.

Within the spaciousness of the prayer and in the light of conscience, a new possibility opens for us. No longer penned in, shadow boxing in the dark, we change. We ourselves become an arena, an open field, where more of who we are is revealed. We begin to pray as we are, not as we wish we might be. When we allow into our consciousness the possibility—if for us it is not yet a felt reality—of God's presence with us, we need not shrink from what clouds and obscures that presence. Our darkness and our light both belong to God. Christ gave us the Lord's Prayer to lead us into the kingdom, to unite us to him and to each other. There is no need to change before we come to him; it is he that is waiting to change us.

As we approach the Lord's Prayer, we need not fear either seeing ourselves or being seen. Martin Luther reminds us that in all true prayer we must feel our distress, and that in the prayer itself is set out the "distress which ought to concern us most." We all have great failings and great needs, but the greatest of all is that they are neither felt nor sensed. The Lord's Prayer unveils these needs in us and bids us, as Luther says, "plead such necessities and wants, not because He does not know them, but that you may kindle your heart to stronger and greater desires, and make wide and open your cloak to receive much." When self-knowledge is supported and enlightened by the Lord's Prayer, we come to feel both our deepest need and the nature of its fulfillment. We see ourselves as we are and yet are not led into despair or guilt, for we do not watch alone or pray alone but in the love and mercy of the Father.

RESISTING: HIDING FROM THE LIGHT

Another aspect of the prayer as an awakener of conscience is that, said attentively, the prayer searches out our hearts. How closely do we conform to each petition? A sixth-century father of the Eastern Church, John Climacus, said of the Lord's Prayer that "it is a judgment when only one word contains the shadow of a lie." We may sense dimly that indeed we do not conform to the word of God as revealed in the prayer. As our encounter grows deeper, perception is sharpened, and we see more clearly who we are and who we are called to be. There may be a subtle resistance to having this disparity exposed, revealed under a holy and implacable light.

We pray, "Thy kingdom come," but are we ready to receive it? As we pray for the coming of the kingdom, are we ourselves at this moment stony ground or fertile soil? We ask forgiveness as we forgive others, but we may become aware of an entrenched attitude of resentment, a habit of harboring bitterness against those who have offended us. The resistance to allowing these observations to appear to us is often unconscious, but such evasion is one of the underlying attitudes that prevent us from listening with full attention to the Lord's Prayer.

We recoil from the judgment of which Climacus speaks. When sensed attentively in prayer, however, this judgment does not condemn us, but instead awakens us to what we lack. It creates in us not guilt but a vivifying remorse. As Luther says, it "kindles" our desires, in order that "you might make wide and open your cloak to receive much." This is the change the prayer brings about in us. It leads us not to improvement but to *metanoia,* repentance, a radical uprooting and reorientation at the very center of the Christian path. "Repentance is a fruit of the Holy Spirit," writes French Cistercian abbot André Louf, "and one of the most trustworthy indications of his operation in the soul. No one can get to know his or her sin without at the same time getting to know God *not before or afterwards, but simultaneously in one and the same moment of spiritual insight.*"

When our listening shows us how far we are from being who the prayer calls us to be, we are allowing the prayer to act upon us. We are no longer resisting. We are witnessing ourselves from an entirely new perspective in which judgment is irrelevant. Attending to the Lord's Prayer has moved us from one level to another, where such vision is possible. In this state, we do not judge ourselves and feel guilty. Instead we see and are seen; both sense our need for mercy and receive it.

Over time, the prayer may "escape" the allotted time of prayer and begin to appear in our lives. This effect may not be a continuum so much as an irruption. Suddenly we are aware that what lies before us is a choice. We understand for a moment that we are free beings, free to choose one way or another—to speak, or not; to give of ourselves, or not, to return and remember, or to turn away. We see that the Lord's

Prayer speaks now and always, and that our need to watch and to pray is ceaseless.

Because the prayer is so familiar, the reality of the Master teaching it to us sometimes fades. To imagine that we are being taught the prayer in the moment—that we are listening to the prayer as Christ is teaching it to each one of us—awakens our feeling and deepens our sensitivity. Listening in this way, we become more porous and receptive: from the very first words, "Our Father," the Father is with us, he hears us, and responds.

REACHING: TRYING TO TRAP GOD

Resistance to experiencing the truth about ourselves can melt away in the healing fire of remorse. But this resistance is not the only barrier to our listening. For most of us there will be times when we will experience a sense of strain, as though it were up to us to bridge a great distance. The Lord's Prayer is majestic, and our concerns seem trivial. We are small, we feel, and God is great and seems far away. At such times it is tempting to reach out, to raise our voices, as it were, to make sure we will be heard. This is childish and naïve, of course, but it comes from the long habit of wishing to *do* something. While listening to the Lord's Prayer, become aware of this strain. See if this trying to "reach God" is there, and be alert to its recurrence.

One scholar has pointed out that the root meaning of *prayer* in Aramaic is "to lay a trap." But we don't lay a trap for God: to the contrary, we must allow ourselves to be snared. H. E. Fosdick writes that if we fail to find God real, often it is because we are seeking God—we will not be prepared to experience God's presence until we realize that God is seeking us. We turn the parable upside down, he says: "According to our attitude in prayer the shepherd is lost, and the sheep have gone out on the tempest-driven mountainside to search for him."

We may read again and again that God is within us, waiting, closer than our inmost self, but such knowledge does not take us very far. We sense a barrier, a blockage. We try to pray, but this very trying creates tension and anxiety. Teresa of Avila speaks of the futility of placing trust in her own efforts:

> Prayer and trust. I used indeed to pray for help. But I now see that I committed the fatal mistake of not putting my whole trust in His Majesty. I should have utterly and thoroughly distrusted, detested, and suspected myself. I sought help. I sometimes took great pains to get it. But I did not understand how little use all that is until we root out all confidence out of ourselves and place it once and forever, absolutely, in God. Those were eighteen miserable years.

Not the work of a day, this rooting out of our trust in ourselves and our abilities, even for a saint. But it can begin by watching in prayer for the moment when we take things into our own hands and try to make something happen. "Let us rest content," advises Baron von

Hügel; "we have not to invent God nor to hold him. He holds us."

Listening to the Lord's Prayer calls us to a willed not-doing, a passivity that at the same time demands a moment-to-moment alert attention that refuses nothing, invents nothing. "Forgive me for having tried to evoke Your presence in my own silence," writes Thomas Merton. "It is you Who must create me within your own silence! Only this newness can save me from idolatry!" The tendency to want to be in control, to insist on the experience we think we know and expect to happen closes us to a far more subtle and unknown realm of experience. The Lord's Prayer brings finer impresssions to us, and it asks us to become attuned and receptive to this utterly new and unfamiliar realm.

It is because the movements of the Spirit are subtle and silent that we are told to watch and be vigilant. Meditative prayer demands of us a quiet and calm attention. If we think of spiritual experience as dramatic and striking, we may disregard the true movement of the Spirit within, which may be—literally—beneath our notice.

An anonymous writer of the mid-twentieth century cautioned that "he who aspires to authentic spiritual experience never confounds the *intensity* of the experience undergone with the *truth* that is revealed—or is not revealed—through it." In other words, he continues,

he does not regard the *force* of impact of an inner experience as a criterion of its authenticity and truth. For an illusion . . . can bowl you over, while a true revelation from above can take place in the guise of a scarcely perceptible inner whispering. Far from imposing itself through force, authentic spiritual experience sometimes requires very awake and very concentrated attention so as not to let it pass by unnoticed. . . . As a general rule, the spiritual world does not at all resemble the surging of the sea—at work to break down the dams holding it back, so as to inundate the land. No, what characterizes the spiritual world, i.e. the "sphere of the Holy Spirit," is the consideration that it has for the human condition. The amount and frequency of revelation from above, destined for a human being, is measured with a lot of care, so as to avoid every possible perturbation in the moral and physical equilibrium of this person.

Just as we need not reach and strain, we need not be apprehensive or uneasy. As we attend to the Lord's Prayer, most of the responses and resonances we perceive will be pitched to our capacities of the moment. But they will be in the unaccustomed language of silence or a "barely perceptible inner whispering." How do we become attuned to these resonances? How, in practice, do we become "essential hearers" of the word as it discloses itself to us? Dietrich Bonhoeffer says, "The words which come from God will be the steps upon which we find our way to God."

Let us turn to the words of the Lord's Prayer.

CHAPTER 3

Our Father who art in heaven:

Turning Homeward

Are you on very sure ground when you begin the Lord's Prayer? Is it clear to you what you mean when you call upon our Father? It is a spiritual Father, a heavenly Father that we call upon, certainly, but is Father just another name for God, one of many possible descriptions? God is called the Absolute, the Almighty, the One: why is it that Christ spoke of the Father, and to the Father? In what sense are we "children" of the Father?

Does it seem to you naïve, in a time of space travel and string theory, to call on God the Father? It was offensive to many when Jesus called God Father—does it offend you? Does it mean to you that God is male?

The history of Christianity is rife with harmful authoritarian and patriarchal attitudes and policies perpetrated in the name of the fatherhood of God, causing many of us to shrink from calling upon the Father.

It seems that misunderstandings about—and misappropriations of—the divine name *Father* have been with us from the moment Jesus declared the fatherhood of God. Parables about the kingdom of God do much to enlighten us as we will see later. But meanwhile here are two examples, one from the Gospel and one from Hugh of Balma, a thirteenth-century Carthusian abbot that may help us now.

We all know the story of the prodigal son. Jan Milic Lochman directs our attention to the father in the parable. "Against all prevailing laws and customs he does not stand in his son's way but lets him go," he writes, ". . . and when the prodigal returns crushed, the father does not count up and expect repayment but runs to meet him. The father runs: an unheard-of action in the patriarchal code. But this unheard-of feature in the father's attitude characterizes the New Testament concept. It cuts right across all pagan and pseudo-Christian ideas of God. . . . This Father who meets us nonjudgmentally is not an extension of the patriarchal and authoritarian mentality and order, but a challenge to it."

The divine Father does not punish his lost son as expected—the son after all hopes at best to be treated as one of his father's hirelings—but instead filled with joy at his homecoming runs to meet him. The parable illuminates a new relationship. Like the father in the parable, our Father in heaven does not bind us to him but freely releases us, awaiting our free return. When we say the first words of the Lord's Prayer the parable asks us: "Are you still in exile? Have you yet begun to turn homeward?" Each time we begin the prayer we can find ourselves within the parable—lost in forgetfulness or beginning to remember again. The Father waits for our return, to ourselves and to him. And wherever we are, the Father who awaits us is not in the least like an authoritarian judge but is instead what Hugh of Balma called a "seed of deifying love." When we turn and seek him, we find we are already in his embrace

Perhaps it is worth pausing now to remind ourselves that while God is the Creator of all life, Christians are *adopted* as children of the Father. Creatures of the creator by nature, we are not yet sons and daughters. Christ is the only Son who is "begotten not made." But Christ bids us call God Father, "my Father and your Father." Christ calls us to be his brothers and sisters and in so doing bridges the great gap between God and humanity. He gives us a way: "I am the way and the truth and the life. . . . " It is not by nature, but through adoption and grace, through Christ and the Holy Spirit, that we become sons and daughters—"When we cry, Abba! Father! it is that very Spirit bearing witness with our spirit that we are children of God" (Romans 8:15-16).

When Hugh of Balma refers to the Father as the "seed of deifying love" we are again far from authoritarian power structures. From this seed, Hugh continues, "which richly radiates life from on high, the human spirit receives sensation and spiritual stirring that truly attest to the sources of life." The human spirit "is fortified with love as God mercifully shapes and forms her out of his fatherly affection—until in the end she sees him face-to-face. All of this is the hidden, or mystical, significance of saying 'Father'—for he is the fountainhead of all life." This is a Father who draws us to another level and brings us to Christ's avowal that "I came that they may have life, and have it abundantly" (John 10:10). With his advent dawns the fully human life, lived in the sphere of the Father, the Son, and the Holy Spirit.

Ultimately we will find the meaning of Father only in prayer, only in our own intimate encounter, and to do this we must first expose the hidden and barely conscious attitudes and assumptions that impede that encounter. For the word of God to penetrate and reach us the old opinions must be exposed and a holy inner silence established. Only then do we become fertile soil, receptive to "the deifying seed." The insights and experiences of others can help us toward this and open our minds to possibilities for the moment beyond our own capacities. But no one else's experience can substitute for our own. Unless we have our own true experience there will be no common ground where the understanding of others might correspond and take root—no matter how inspiring, no matter how *true,* the words of others will roll over us like water over stone.

COMING HOME

The Lord's Prayer is the prayer of a son or daughter in formation, a prayer made in trust and dependence and with the assurance that it will be heard. It is primarily the prayer of a disciple, and this is where we can make a beginning: if we do not yet have this assurance we pray nonetheless; we pray in obedience, as a disciple. We pray not in blind obedience but relying upon our own response to the words and message of Jesus, even if the response is undeveloped and so deep that we have yet fully to apprehend it, even if we have not yet seen the Father "face-to-face." We remember that it is Jesus who both commands us and empowers us to call upon God as Father. We lay aside our misgivings, our hesitations, our doubts, our lack of faith, our unworthiness, our reservations. We pray the Lord's Prayer because we are commanded to do so and call God Father because as disciples of Christ his sacrifice enables us to do so. We pray to be made true sons and daughters of the Father. This spirit of obedience frees us to pray when we have no inclination, when our muddled efforts and subjective judgment tell us we "aren't getting anywhere." In this same spirit of obedience we set our rule of prayer and commit to begin listening to the Lord's Prayer. Like the prodigal child, we turn our steps homeward.

Each of us sets his or her rule. Whatever time is set aside, come to prayer daily. It is better to begin with a period of ten minutes once a day and be sure of keeping to it than to set a longer rule you are likely to neglect or skip. Fidelity motivated by obedience is a first small step. Make a beginning and set aside your own will in this one matter. In so doing the strength of your self-will will be exposed in a way that it had perhaps not been before. In your decision to obey Christ's instruction you create for yourself a new condition, a condition of conscious choice. It is a sign of inner freedom, for what characterizes freedom more than choice?

Every day then begins anew, and you choose anew— to turn consciously toward freedom or to submit to the forces ready to sweep you irretrievably into the stuff of the day, into submission and servitude to outer demands. This is why for most of us a period of morning prayer is essential, and another period before retiring. Spiritual writers throughout the centuries have also suggested a shorter period at noon if practicable. The ability to choose is a gift. Choose your rule—and obey with joy.

The discipline of daily obedience, of daily fidelity, is universally enjoined upon us. John of the Cross cautions that "he who interrupts the course of his spiritual exercises and prayer is like a man who allows a bird to escape from his hand; he can hardly catch it again." We already know that we can lose our way easily and that it can take a long time before the wish to pray comes to the surface again. It has already been proven to us and yet we all still need reminders. Knowing this, Christ teaches us to pray, "Give us this day our *daily* bread." Each day we need to feed the hidden hunger for real being within us.

We often forget a wish to pray now is not solely a result of our decision. Rather, it comes to us when for a moment we are open to the current of prayer already present within us. André Louf tells us that our true heart is asleep and "has to be woken up gradually— through the course of a whole lifetime. . . . We have to become conscious of what we have already received, must learn to feel, to distinguish it in the full and peaceful assurance of the Spirit, this prayer rooted and operative somewhere deep inside us." If we omit our prayer for even one day we are in danger of falling fast asleep again, and of bringing upon our next beginning more obstacles than we had encountered before. If we think it is our decision to pray or not, that we can stop and begin as we wish, we are in danger of losing the track for many months or even years.

So, to begin your experiment in listening to the Lord's Prayer, set a daily plan. Determine a place where you will be alone and undisturbed. You can sit on a chair or cross-legged on the floor; you can stand or you can kneel. What is important is to find a position that allows the spine to be free and aligned, erect but not rigid, like the stem of a plant oriented to the sun at noon. If you are seated on a chair, the knees should be slightly lower than the hips. The position must be comfortable enough so that the body will be able to remain still during the time of prayer. The fourteenth-century English mystic Richard Rolle quaintly expresses his preference and frees us to choose our own:

I have loved for to sit: for no penance, nor fantasy, nor that I wished men to talk of me, nor for no such thing: but only because I knew that I loved God more and longer lasted within the comfort of love than going, or standing, or kneeling. For sitting I am most at rest, and my heart most upward. But therefore peradventure it is not best that another should sit, as I did and will do to my death, save he were disposed in soul as I was.

Once you have arrived at your time and place begin the first experiment by watching the breath. With eyes slightly open and cast down, or closed, sit quietly for a few moments and begin to count the breathing, from one to ten, and from one to ten again. Watch while the counting goes on. Especially follow the flow of the breath as it enters the nostrils and sense the "hinge" of the breath in the bellows of the abdomen as it changes from the in-breath to the out-breath to the in-breath again. The first claim on your attention is to follow the breathing; the counting is mere accompaniment, a bone thrown to the mind to keep it occupied and pacified until a quieter state establishes itself. Under no circumstances try to change or to slow or to alter the breathing in any way. All our instinctive functions are working optimally and to interfere is harmful. Watch without expectation, without demand. Both expectation and demand push us forward, out of the present.

If counting seems to create tensions, stop counting for a while and follow the breath as it circulates in and out. This counting exercise has no intrinsic importance or value; it is simply a study, a way of seeing how watching—by itself—collects our attention and brings us a little closer to the present moment. If awareness creates a subtle alteration in the breathing, drop it for a time, and rest in a sensation of the weight of your body.

If the breathing changes of itself, allow it to change. If a deep breath comes, let it come. The exercise is simply to prepare a space within. It is a kind of buffer between the stream of our usual state and the dawning state of prayer.

It is important to be reminded that no technique or exercise brings about prayer. In Christian prayer all methods are temporary, dispensable, and unnecessary. As Orthodox Bishop Ignati has written, the state of prayer comes "by God's grace at the proper time which He Himself determines." He adds, "Mechanical methods of a physical kind are suggested by the Fathers exclusively as means to achieve attention in prayer quickly and easily, but not as something essential."

After counting to ten twice, close the eyes if they had been open. Say the first words of the Lord's Prayer either quietly aloud or silently. Listen. Allow the words to resonate for the space of a few breaths, three or four, before saying the next few words. A practical division is: Our Father/who art in heaven/hallowed by thy name/thy kingdom come/thy will be done/on earth as it is in heaven/give us this day our daily bread/and forgive us our debts/as we also have forgiven our debtors/and lead us not into temptation/but deliver us from evil/Amen.

Remember that the whole of the prayer is in the now: you are invoking now, petitioning now, affirming now.

This experiment is intended to slow us down. You may sense the pressure to move to the next phrase quickly. If you find that a few phrases have passed by without stopping, return to the last phrase said with awareness and go on from there. Otherwise say the prayer through once only in this way during each period of prayer. It is a prayer of the whole being, so maintain an awareness of the breathing and of the body as the prayer continues. Notice when the words sound in the mind alone and come back to the awareness of the whole body situated within the radiance of the prayer. Don't try to relax, but notice the release of tensions as they fall away.

Is this meditation, or *lectio divina,* or contemplation? We are beginners, and our experiment is probably none of the above very precisely. But to be troubled by definitions at this early stage will only impede us. Certainly we come with a wish to pray and this wish is in itself of utmost importance. Poet and Jesuit Gerard Manley Hopkins says of prayer that "it is the expression of a wish to God, and since God searches the heart, the conceiving even of the wish to pray is prayer in God's eyes. . . . Corresponding on man's side is not so much corresponding as the wish to correspond, and this least sigh of desire, this one aspiration, is the life and spirit of man."

This wish is fragile and subtle and can be overlooked in the tendency to try to understand, or to try to get something, or to feel something. During the pauses between the phrases all of these tendencies are allowed to be, and in being seen, allowed to fall away. Again, neither reach nor resist. Because we are listening to the word, we can be said to be meditating; because we listen in silence we may experience moments of contemplation. Whatever the description, we have entered into the movement of prayer—watching.

After a week or so of saying the prayer in the way described above, it may be useful to try in the same way adding "Father," before each phrase: Father, thy kingdom come; Father, thy will be done, and so on.

For another period of time the prayer may be tried instead with the addition of "Amen" after each phrase. When a form of exercise is chosen, it should be kept for at least six or eight sessions of prayer.

In whatever way and at whatever time we turn toward the Lord's Prayer it is certain that it will instruct us—we do not have to be clever or learned or particularly distinguished in any way. Swiss mystic Adrienne von Speyr tells us that we behold truth in the word, and that this beholding itself supports us. "God's truth," she writes, "is a truth which reveals, unveils, and proclaims itself; it provides firm ground, expands horizons, reveals insight, removes obstacles and generates an objective light. As a result the person praying can see that he is part of a movement created, not by himself, but by truth, and that his knowledge is not imaginary, originating in himself, but comes from the word of God." This affirms what Kelpius said long ago of the riches of the Lord's Prayer: "experience will teach it you."

Our experience will include periods of frustration and aridity when it seems pointless to continue. On this point spiritual elders are unanimous: these are often far more valuable than times at which we are feeling enlightened, capable, and confident. Persevering in the face of difficulty strips away self-reliance and prepares the way for the deep and simple state of receptivity to which the prayer calls us.

It is worthwhile here to be reminded never to discuss one's experiences in prayer except with a spiritual counselor. Keeping silence about what we encounter shelters our experience. It keeps it hidden from the grasping and self-aggrandizing part of our egotism. If we throw pearls before swine they will indeed trample them underfoot and turn and maul us. Brought up from the depths, our experience when indiscriminately shared can become exteriorized and quickly exploited under all manner of guises.

❧

These first words of the prayer are addressed to the Father, and we know that Jesus used both Father and *abba,* an Aramaic word used by grown-up sons and daughters as well as by little children to address their fathers. According to Joachim Jeremias, a great New Testament scholar who has investigated this term deeply, Jesus' use of *abba* to address God is absolutely original to him and was possible only with his advent. Jeremias writes that "the cry 'Abba!' is beyond all human capabilities, and is only possible within the new relationship with God given by the Son." Macdonald adds that we would not have known the heart of the Father "but for him who cast himself into the gulf that yawned between us."

Because of the incarnation we can join with Christ in saying *abba*. This term, *abba,* we must note, is not a description but an address. We call, we cry, Abba! Father! aware that, as Karl Barth has written, we cannot as Christians properly speak *about* God, but only *to* him. And it is only because of Christ that we can address him with a word so astonishing and so full of mystery. "When we say 'Abba, Father,'" asks Gerhard Eberling, "have we not the fulfillment of all prayer, the presence of the Holy Spirit and the nearness of God? Yet all this is so easily said," he adds, "Till our deathbed we have to work unceasingly at the one lesson: to learn to say with all our heart, 'Abba, Father.'"

Many commentators tell us that the phrase "who art in heaven" is there to remind us that while our Father is near, within, he is also remote. These words bring the majesty and awesome grandeur of God home to us—He is immanent but also transcendent. Jungian Helen Luke finds the "which art in heaven" of the King James Version can signal this intention as well. "'Which'" can be a hint of the essential impersonality of the Father added to his aspect as Person," she writes, "The 'who' can subtly increase the temptation to reduce the Creator from Person to a personality, to the benevolent or frightening all-powerful father figure who will rescue us from our troubles or before whom we cringe in guilt. The prayer starts with a categorical warning against all such anthropomorphizing of God."

Certainly, the call to be sons and daughters does not relegate us to infantile dependency or arrested maturity. And, as Luke cautions, we may be surprised at how often our reactions belie these unconscious attitudes. It would seem that God-is-on-my-side fanaticism and all manner of pagan propitiations spring from this misunderstanding of "Father." But for all this we must not put him too far off, advises Gerhard Ebeling. "To proclaim God as the God who is near, as Jesus did, is to put an end to the idea of God's distant dwelling place and to reverse the relation of God and heaven. It is not that where heaven is, there is God, but that where God is, there is heaven." Better to stop thinking of heaven altogether, he concludes, if by so doing we are in danger of losing the heart of Christ's teaching.

The persistent habit of thinking about heaven as a place "up there" was tackled head on by the anonymous writer of *The Cloud of Unknowing* in the fourteenth century. His young disciples hear that they are to "lift up their hearts to God" and he observes them begin to gaze skyward, "as if they hoped to catch the heavenly songs of angels. In another place, he describes youths who, hoping for the food of angels, are "in the habit of gaping openmouthed as though they were trying to catch flies."

That Christ ascended upward is incidental to the spiritual reality, this writer adds. "For in the realm of the spirit heaven is as near up as it is down, behind as before, or left or to right. . . . The path to heaven is measured by desire and not by miles. . . . We need not strain our spirit in all directions to reach heaven, for we dwell there already through love and desire." Again, heaven is not where God is, but where God is, there is heaven. As we move through the horizontal dimension of time, heaven is the vertical dimension of the now, eternally rooted in the Father.

⁜

Another fundamental word stands at the beginning of the Lord's Prayer: "Our." Standing at the beginning it tacitly accompanies each petition. It has been said that in the Lord's Prayer the "I" is silent. We don't pray alone, on our own behalf, but with and on behalf of others. We remember all beings, all creatures that accompany us here on earth, the earth itself, the "living, the dead, and the yet unborn," in the words of one ancient prayer. Christ teaches us to say "our," and implicates us in the Father's creation. He teaches us that our being in its very nature is shared being; each being is inextricably knit into the substance of all being and sustained by the same love. The isolating subjectivity that makes us forget this reality is shaken each time the Lord's Prayer bids us say "our," and "us."

We allow ourselves to be shaken. We watch in prayer, and as we sit in silence after saying the first words of the prayer, we are asked, "Whom do you reject?" Which persons? What groups? The question is inescapable. The prayer instructs and searches us out from the start. It acts on us in a way that we may find difficult to welcome but nonetheless cannot deny. Christ commands us to say "*Our* Father."

Alfred Delp wrote from his prison cell that in these words suddenly the chasm between us is spanned: "The common center, the personal God who speaks to us and to whom we speak, makes mankind human and the community a genuine whole." Every one of us is human; every one is our neighbor, part of the same body. Christ asks us to see his face in the face of our neighbor. Simeon the New Theologian wrote in the tenth century that "'you gave me food,' 'you gave me drink,' 'you clothed me,' and so on does not indicate one incident, but *a constant attitude to everyone.*"

The Lord's Prayer acts to instill this understanding within us now, in the present, and because this understanding must be constant so must it be constantly renewed. "Do not think that one renewal of life, once for all, so to speak is sufficient," wrote Origen, "rather forever and ever, and every day, if one may say so, the newness itself is for renewing. As the apostle says, 'Though the outward part of our nature is being worn down, our inner life is refreshed from day to day.'"

As beginners we have an advantage, an advantage that we must strive to keep as we pray. Let us go on, unknowing, with newness itself renewing in us.

CHAPTER 4

Hallowed be thy name:

From the Imaginary to the Real

The Lord's Prayer begins by calling upon the Father and entrusting ourselves to his infinite care. Then come the words: "Hallowed be thy name." Suddenly an unfathomable vastness appears. We become a tiny speck, seemingly invisible, and far from the ranks of angels and saints that sing, "Holy, holy, holy, Lord God of Hosts! Heaven and earth are full of thy glory." In a blinding radiance that is darkness to our weak eyes we sense our exile, our separation, and our nothingness: we are not able, we are not worthy to be a part of the heavenly chorus. But Christ teaches us in the Lord's Prayer that here on earth, despite all, we are invited to join in adoration and praise, and that adoration is at the center of our being.

In the third century Tertullian wrote, "The whole creation prays. Cattle and wild beasts pray, and bend their knees, and in coming forth from their stalls and lairs look up to heaven, their mouths not idle, making the spirit move in their own fashion. Moreover the birds taking flight lift themselves up to heaven, and instead of hands, spread out the cross of their wings, while saying something which may be supposed to be a prayer." It is a prayer of praise: "Glory to thee, O God, glory to thee," sings the whole creation.

This praise comes naturally to us. It springs up from within: "Everything that breathes, praise the Lord," bids the psalmist. We do not need to create this praise, or stir it up, or incite it. If we are insensible of it, it is because we are too noisy. Strangely, the more purely we experience this inherent state of praise, the more silence descends upon us. Thought recedes, the body is still, feeling is set ablaze. "God is silence," said Abraham of Napthar in the sixth century, "and in silence is he sung and glorified." This is not exterior silence, he adds, nor the silence of the tongue or of the body or of the soul, but of the spirit. "The silence of the spirit is when all its movements are stirred solely by Being; in this state it is truly silent, aware that the silence which is upon it is itself silent." This silence is far from us, but any effort toward it pushes it further away. We pray "Hallowed be thy name," and the silence approaches us. We see a new direction—not idle silence but active silence, alert to an intrinsic upwelling of praise. Praise is no more an effort than breathing is. Breathing and praise flow together, as one.

We have become dulled by custom, our minds narrowed by the one-pointed view of materialism, our souls hardened through lack of nourishment, but praise is inherent despite all this. "From the moment when we first come into contact with the world," observes Scottish writer George MacDonald, "it is to us a revelation of God." He goes on to contrast the scientific description of water with the direct apprehension of it:

> There is no water in oxygen, no water in hydrogen; it comes bubbling fresh from the imagination of the living God, rushing from under the great white throne of the glacier. The very thought of it makes one gasp with an elemental joy no metaphysician can analyze. The water itself, that dances, and sings, and slakes the wonderful thirst—symbol and picture of that draught for which the woman of Samaria made her prayer to Jesus—this lovely thing itself, whose very wetness is a delight to every inch of the human body in its embrace—this live thing which, if I might, I would have running through my room, yea, babbling along my table—this water is its own self, its own truth, and is therein a truth of God. Let him who would know the love of the Maker become sorely athirst, and drink of the brook by the way—then lift up his heart, not at that moment to the maker of oxygen and hydrogen, but to the inventor and mediator of thirst and water, that man might foresee a little of what his soul may find in God.

Who reading this is not stirred to gladness and thanksgiving? Praise springs spontaneously from the awakened soul.

IN THE LIGHT OF GLORY

In the eighteenth century, Benjamin Franklin felt the need to modernize the language of the Lord's Prayer. In regard to this phrase of the prayer he wrote,

> The Word *hallowed* is almost obsolete: People now have but an imperfect Conception of the Meaning of the Petition. It is therefore proposed to change the Expression into: *May all revere thee.*

This effort to "improve" the Lord's Prayer was not widely adopted, but it provides a useful starting point to think about the petition. It will help us move from the outside in. Most of us, after all, are among those who have "but an imperfect Conception" of the meaning of "hallowed be thy name." Does it mean to honor the name of God in all we do? Is it a kind of amplification of the commandment not to "take the name of the LORD thy God in vain"? Dictionary definitions of *hallowed* include "set apart, highly venerated," as in "hallowed ground." In the prayer, then, are we being instructed, as Franklin suggests, simply to venerate the name of the Lord? Do most of us glide over this phrase, make a quick inner genuflection, and move on? Do we call on the Father, grant him reverence, and *then* begin to pray?

Franklin was right—"hallowed" is an almost obsolete word—but his paraphrase of the petition falls far short of its full meaning. Commentators have said that in this phrase we have reached the "heart and kernel of Christ's message," that in this phrase is the "essence" of the prayer. Does it seem so to us as we pray?

It comes as a surprise to most of us to learn that the petition is not primarily about human activity, but about the activity of God. Lord's Prayer scholar Nicholas Ayo writes, "The Father is glorified by God's work in us, and not by our independent initiative before God." In this phrase and throughout the prayer we are asking *God* to act. In grammatical terms, the phrase is in a tense that demands an action be done now, at this moment, once and for all, and asks for this with urgency. The next two petitions of the prayer, in the same tense, are translated literally:

Come, the kingdom of you
Be done, the will of you

But "be hallowed, the name of you," doesn't communicate much more to us than "hallowed be thy name." Commentators on the prayer concur that hallowed means "glorified." Certainly, Jesus' abiding dedication to the glory of the Father is evident throughout the Gospel—that the Father's glory might be recognized is indeed the beginning and end of Christ's mission, the "heart and kernel" of his teaching, and so we seem to be drawing nearer to his intention.

Following the construction of the above petitions, then, with verb first, we see that literally this phrase can be translated

Be manifest, the glory of you.

We are asking that the glory of the Father be made manifest now. We pray that this be so. "On earth as it is in heaven" applies to all three of the petitions preceding, and so we pray that just as the glory of the Father is fully manifest in heaven, so may it be fully manifest here on earth. We call on God, urgently, to reveal his glory. "God's present glory, his supreme holiness and majesty here and now, are Christ's single and immediate concern," observes theologian Heinz Schürmann. And so Christ, right at the beginning of the prayer, calls us to desire what he desires, to pray that God might be all in all—that the glory of the name of the Father be manifest here and now. Would not even an infinitesimal reflection of his glory bring us to an awed and profoundly reverential silence?

If our eyes are opened, if we see the glory of the Father, we cannot but desire his kingdom and wish to conform to his will. And only when we recognize his glory do we join in adoration with our whole being: "Holy, holy, holy, the Lord God the Almighty, who was and is and is to come" (Revelation 4:8).

Nothing we do can take away from or add to the holiness of the Father. That the Father's name is hallowed is reality itself, and so, as Simone Weil writes, "to ask for that which exists . . . infallibly, eternally, and quite independent of our prayer, that is the perfect petition. . . . We cannot prevent ourselves from desiring; we are made of desire; but the desire that nails us down to what is imaginary, temporal, selfish, can, if we make it pass wholly into this petition, become a lever to tear us from the imaginary into the real, and from time into eternity, to lift us right out of the prison of self."

The prayer, we begin to discern, is a long journey. We are just beginning. And here, at the outset, Christ instructs us to turn confidently to our Father in heaven and confess our blindness. We can't see, we are imprisoned in our dreams, confused, and unable to perceive the reality that underlies our entire visible world. Our Father, we pray, make manifest your glory to us now. Only in the light of this glory do we take the next steps, to desire his kingdom and his will. Only in the grace of this light is faith born. "What is the hallowing of the name of God other than the incoming of the Holy Spirit?" asks a ninth-century abbot. And how is faith born but by the breath of the Holy Spirit within?

Even a glimpse of the Father's glory awakens us. It is this glimpse that transmutes our desire into a wish to correspond to what has been revealed. Through this glimpse, in our minds and hearts is born the wish that this glory might be manifest concretely—within us, among us, and through us. The eye of conscience is opened and guides us and the hallowing of the name is reflected in our attitude toward our neighbor and toward all creation. "Prayer and service are an indivisible unity," writes Adrienne von Speyr, "a unity of watchfulness, readiness, self-offering, and the attempt to bear and carry out what one has received."

A LIVING SILENCE

The prayer reminds us that in everything, we are to ask God to act within us; that our part is to become present so that we may be available and vulnerable. It is difficult to remember that God's activity does not begin when we begin to pray or come to an end when our prayer ends. He does not vanish when we turn away. And we cannot force or somehow induce his presence. The lever that tears us, in Weil's words, "from the imaginary into the real" is our attentiveness and not our "doing." It is important to bear in mind that the experiments suggested earlier do not bring into being the silence wherein we listen. Silence "is already there," writes a Carthusian,

> and it is simply a matter of letting it rise from within so that it eliminates by its very presence the noise that distracts or invades us. . . . Once we have heard this silence we thirst to hear it again. We must, however, free ourselves from the idea that we can of ourselves reproduce it. It is there; it is always there even if we no longer hear it. . . . Silence is a listening: not the feverish expectation of a word that would strike our ears or fill our heart, but a calm receptivity to him who is present and who works noiselessly in our inmost being. . . . Listening to the Lord is no

longer then an activity of the intelligence or the sensibility, but a sort of communion of our whole being with the presence of him who sustains it and communicates life in love.

Exercises of breathing or counting or pausing during the Lord's Prayer therefore are not intended to muffle the inner chatter that the Buddhists call "monkey mind," or to suppress agitation and tension. Instead, their aim is to alert us to a field of vibration already present, a living silence out of which the words of the prayer emanate and in which they resound. The silence we enter is not and cannot be imposed. It is instead the deeply informing silence of the Father.

There is of course an effort we must undertake to understand the meaning of the words of the prayer. But we must be reminded again and again that while this effort to ponder and to understand is essential, at the time of prayer concepts and ideas are put aside, even ideas and concepts about the prayer. New knowledge comes to each one only in silence, and thinking about one's own ideas or those of others will only impede this new understanding, not enhance it. The word and silence alternate—but not our words nor an enforced silence.

"The head is a crowded rag market," writes Russian Orthodox monk Theophan the Recluse. "All those who want to establish one thought of God within themselves, are advised to leave the head and descend with their mind into their heart, and to stand there with ever-present attention." The aim of all Orthodox prayer is to "find the place of the heart," to "unite the mind with the heart," to "gather the attention in the heart." If prayer is in the mind alone, it is not true prayer; this comes only when body, mind, and heart are all united. And if the mind has not yet descended from head to heart, one Orthodox spiritual advisor suggests that, whether we speak the words of prayer aloud or not, we be aware of them sounding in the throat, a shift of attention downward that helps relate head and body and prepares the way to the heart.

We are turning aside from our usual paths when we begin to pray, and that is why we may experience subtle fears and resistance. We submit to an unfamiliar authority within and enter into an unknown realm. Whether suddenly, in a moment, or slowly over time, it is only as our familiar coordinates fall away in an awareness of the Father's presence that we are led truly to pray, "Hallowed be thy name."

CHAPTER 5

Thy kingdom come:

The Mysterious Fullness

We are more at home here than anywhere in the prayer. "Thy kingdom come," we pray, and it doesn't trouble us that we are not sure of its exact meaning. When Jesus bids us call God our Father, he reveals that our nature is rooted in the divine and shares the divine nature. When he speaks of the kingdom of heaven, he awakens a longing within us for a kingdom we cannot but keenly anticipate. We may be exiles from the kingdom of heaven, but it is where we belong. When we pray, "Thy kingdom come," we are looking back and ahead, both wishing to remember and return and longing for the kingdom to break out among us. We are asking for the fulfillment of our deepest desire, and we sense it.

Still, the kingdom of God is a mystery—not like the kingdoms of earth but nonetheless a kingdom meant to be established on earth. Not a place—"The kingdom of God is not coming with things that can be observed; nor will they say, 'Look, here it is!' or 'There it is!' For in fact, the kingdom of God is among you." Jesus tells us it is like leaven in flour that transforms; like a mustard seed, a tiny speck that nonetheless has the power to grow into a place of shelter and safety; like a pearl or a treasure buried in a field—we stumble across it, yet it is worth all we have. It is dynamic, free, here, coming. We are dazzled and drawn. It is our hope, and we yearn for it.

Romano Guardini illustrates the kingdom at work in his description of Francis of Assisi:

> The kingdom of God surrounds Francis with openness, a holy nearness, a rich, active fullness. He is utterly human; he is human in a particularly beautiful and profound sense in that God works in him unhindered. But around him the world is different from what it is around others. Legends are told of him, but is it really so important whether the birds came to him or not; or whether the fish listened to him; or whether the wolf of Gubbio laid its paw in his hand? That such things could be told of him, though, is proof that around him everything was different from its ordinary self. For the kingdom of God had been able to reach him.
>
> It did not reach him once and for all, but did so anew again and again. With him, the kingdom of God

was not something finished and arrested. With him, too, it was in a state of continuous coming; and if Francis had regarded himself as perfect and had settled down to a state of fixed possession, he would have lost the most precious thing he had. The mysterious fullness that Christ calls the kingdom of God streamed in to him continually. And continually he opened himself to it and received it anew.

SPIRIT STREAMING INTO THE WORLD

Until the coming again of Christ in glory, the fulfilling of the kingdom is carried by the Holy Spirit inflowing into all creation. This streaming of the Spirit into the world is active and pervasive, but is it able to reach us as it reached Francis? In this question lies all our fear, all our struggle, all our anguish. We know the kingdom is near, but we seem far from it. We are asked to serve, to work to hasten the coming of the kingdom, yet we know that all our ideas about how to do this are at their arising inextricably mixed with self-interest and vainglory. They are directed from the inside out in the case of "works" on behalf of others, and from the outside in when we strive for self-improvement. In both instances we are self-oriented and self-directed. We know we are far from the kingdom.

In some ancient texts, "thy kingdom" or "thy reign" come is replaced by "thy Spirit come." In this version we have a reminder, writes Eugraph

Kovalevsky, that it is not only a societal organization or arrangement that this petition anticipates. "Christ says that the 'Kingdom of heaven' is in you and among you," writes Kovalevsky, "as a 'breath of life,' *in* society and *in* us." He suggests we imagine the coming of the Spirit as a new atmosphere, a new environment. "So when we utter the words, 'Thy Kingdom come,'" he adds, "let us begin by thinking: thy climate, the divine climate surround us, may the divine atmosphere (the Holy Spirit) penetrate us."

It is within this atmosphere that we are able to pray in truth the petitions that follow. Only when permeated by the "atmosphere" and under the guidance of the Holy Spirit do we authentically seek the will of God, receive our daily bread, forgive others. Not in the future, but now.

The kingdom has already come with the advent of Christ and is—within time, on earth—ceaselessly coming. The ever-renewed coming of the kingdom to us is the fulfillment of our hope; it is what answers our longing and our desire. One day it will permeate every atom; all will be transfigured, and all will be under the glorious dominion of the Father. This is what we pray may come. Although it is not "of the world," the coming kingdom means that God will transform the world we love, bringing a new heaven and a new earth, making all things new. Christ tells us we can share in this fullness as it is coming, today, now, "on earth as in heaven." He offers it to each one at each moment.

With the advent of Christ, time itself has a new meaning. We are waiting for a future realization, but we are also offered a present fulfillment. We pray that we be made able to perceive the inflowing of the Spirit streaming toward us. Augustine tells us that just as a bright light is absent to the blind or to those who close their eyes, so is the kingdom of God, though ever present on earth, absent to those who are not conscious of it.

Pierre Teilhard de Chardin invites us to open our eyes:

> All around us, to right and left, in front and behind, above and below, we have only to go a little beyond the frontier of sensible appearances in order to see the divine welling up and showing through. . . . By means of all created things, without exception, the divine assails us, penetrates us and moulds us. We imagined it as distant and inaccessible, whereas in fact we live steeped in its burning layers. *In eo vivimus.* As Jacob said, awakening from his dream, the world, this palpable world, which we were wont to treat with the boredom and disrespect with which we habitually regard places with no sacred association for us, is in truth a holy place, and we did not know it. *Venite, adoremus.*

Even if we can't see as clearly as he, we respond. Is it memory? Is it indeed because "the divine assails us, penetrates us and moulds us" whether or not we are able to experience the subtle movement consciously? Even in our ignorance we know *something,* and wish to be able to be at one with what is now just intimation. What keeps us from the coming of the Spirit?

GATHERED TOGETHER

"When two or three of you are gathered in my name, I am there," Christ tells us. Surely this directs us to a life lived in communion and sympathy with each other.

"The whole person, writes Kallistos Ware, "is a person who is on the one side open to God, and on the other side open to other human persons. . . . We become truly personal by loving God and loving other humans. By love, I don't mean merely an emotional feeling, but a fundamental attitude. In its deepest sense, love is the life, the energy, of God himself in us."

We are not true human beings when we are isolated, and when we are closed in on ourselves we are able to perceive very little. Attending to the Lord's Prayer we open, and enter into a current that leads us to God and to others. We are taught to see that our shared being is a fact, not an aim or achievement. We share the same substance, vibrate at the same frequency, and are sustained by the same love of the Father.

To be open to God or to another we must be present, "gathered together" in another sense—within ourselves. "Who are those to be gathered together?" asked an early Father of the Church. He answered in a way difficult to understand: he said it was "the intellect, the will, and the memory." We are to gather together faculties that are usually not united, that live without connection to one another. We usually associate the intellect and the memory, but here they are clearly not the same. Intellect we may assume is mind and reason, but the memory lies in another, deeper realm. It is the mysterious memory that makes the prodigal son "come to himself." Gregory the Sinaite says that our "single and simple memory" has been split up into thoughts and has thus "lost the memory of God." "If I am going to have a true memory," writes Thomas Merton, "there are a thousand things that must first be forgotten. . . . A memory that is not alive to the present does not 'remember' the here and now, does not 'remember' its identity, is not memory at all."

When mind is "gathered together" with this deep memory, when the attention of the mind is open to the activity of this memory, we come to ourselves. And what is the will but a wish to maintain this new opening and this new unity?

The Lord's Prayer is an instrument meant to gather our intellect, our will, and our memory together. We must be attentive as we listen to the prayer, and so it calls the attention of the mind to the present. As we listen, it arouses the will, or the wish, to remain present and open. It awakens our deep memory, reminding us of who we are. It directs our desire toward the coming kingdom and the will of God, toward life that is at one with the Father. Only thus "gathered together," more related within, are we ourselves present. Only then, when we truly appear, is it possible for us to be "on the one side open to God, and on the other side open to other human persons."

Many are troubled by a lack of belief, which they take to mean a lack of faith. But faith cannot be a matter of the mind or intellect alone. Thomas Merton said that faith "perfects the mind"—the mind does not and cannot bring us faith. It is faith, he writes, that "puts the intellect in possession of Truth which reason cannot grasp by itself." Reason alone can go very far astray, and we must beware the belief of the mind when it is unrelated to the whole being. Without a connection to the deep memory and wish, mind-belief is simply fanaticism. It is grounded in nothing but self-will and self-reliance. This kind of belief masquerading as faith is utterly alien to Christ's teaching and to the prayer he gave us. The mind, watching in his prayer, is indeed slowly led and "enlightened"—"put in possession of a Truth which reason alone cannot grasp." This fructifying faith is a gift of the Lord's Prayer.

As we quietly carry on the practice of prayer with the Our Father, we become sensitive to a realm of subtle impressions. Our discrimination is called upon, particularly in relation to the experiments we may be trying. If before beginning to pray the counting seems unnecessary, drop it and allow silence to spread and deepen. If "held" for a longer time at a particular phrase, ignore the pressure to go on, and remain calmly watching. We must follow the subtle impressions that come and beware of trying to direct or manipulate the experience.

A SLOWLY DAWNING LIGHT

Intellect, will, memory—to watch, to wish, to remember—are for most of us newly discovered realms. We are beginners, finding our way. We have no need of big experiences. If they come, they do not prove that one or another of us is better, more worthy, more spiritually talented, more surely called, more fit for the spiritual life, more deserving. Such experiences indeed may become obstacles. A tendency to seek them again can cause us to miss what is being newly brought before us. And they can engender a particularly insidious form of spiritual pride that separates us from our companions. Let us not seek such experiences, or speak of them if they come. A slowly dawning light suits us far better than a blinding one. As we read earlier, a true revelation from above most often takes place in the guise of a "scarcely perceptible inner whispering." It is this inner whispering we are to be listening for, listening with all the attention and care we can.

When we watch and pray, "Thy kingdom come" alerts us to a longing within. This longing may seem to be reaching us as if from a great distance or depth. It may indeed be "scarcely perceptible," but we can be sure it is there. Let us henceforth lean toward this longing within us as we pray, allowing it to be part of our awareness without forcing or trying to amplify it. Our attention enlarges to encompass it, just as it encompasses our breathing and the field of vibration in and around our bodies.

The fourteenth-century German mystic Johannes Tauler spoke of this inner "gathering together." In all creatures endowed with reason, Tauler said, God finds room for the "faithful and fatherly accomplishment of his noble, pure work." It is the Father's work, not our own, yet we must bring ourselves before him. The kingdom of God is actually in the inmost depths of the human being,

> when, with all industry, man draws the outward man into the inward reason-governed man, and these two, that is the powers of sense and reason, enter with mutual accord into the inmost man of all, that is, into the seclusion of the spirit where the true divine image lies, and all at once attains to the divine abyss of God in which he has dwelt forever, uncreated. When merciful God finds man attentive to him in all his candidness and simplicity, the divine fatherly abyss of God bows down and sinks into the candid, attentive depth of man and there reforms his created depth and draws it into his non created Being, so that the candid spirit of man be one with him.

This is the kingdom of God that should be sought first, he says, "in which high state all cares fall away." Our created and uncreated natures are, in the words of Julian of Norwich, "oned with God." Divisions are done away with, and multiplicities reconciled. We are re-formed in the "fatherly abyss of God." Nothing is cast aside, nothing abandoned: with the coming of the kingdom, all is gathered together.

When "with all industry" we begin to withdraw from the tendency of the senses to seek outer stimulation we are beginning the journey of which Tauler speaks. When the "powers of sense and reason" begin to turn inward and we attend quietly to an inner silence, we take another step. Beyond this we are led.

CHAPTER 6

*Thy will be done on
earth as it is in heaven:*

The Divine
and Unassailable
Liberty

On our own infinitesimal scale, we are said to
be made "in the image of God." Let us look
at what *we* intend for the living things we
love. When we sow a seed, we wish it to grow into a
healthy plant, a plant that bears fruit or flowers abundantly, or sends its roots deep and branches high in the
air, according to its nature. If we love a child, we wish
to see all his or her talents and gifts developed, we wish
that a way is found for what is potential in the child to
become manifest. We feel the same toward our friends,
our spouse, any work to which we are committed, our
community, our nation, our world as a whole.

The Lord's Prayer undergirds and supports this well-wishing, this good will toward the entire created realm. It teaches us to ask for the glory of God to shine forth, leading us all to praise him and thank him for our lives and for his love that holds all in being. It teaches us to trust and depend upon him as Father, and to pray that the world come under his gracious authority. Now we are asked to pray that his plan be fulfilled, that as the will of the Father is done in heaven so may it be done on earth.

To say "It's God's will" when feeling abandoned and without hope is to be not only impious but sadly mistaken. How could we imagine the will of the Father—on a scale and level inconceivably higher and greater than our own, encompassing as it does the *alpha* and the *omega,* the beginning and end of all creation—in any instance, under any circumstances, opposed to the current of love and being we ourselves are part of and participate in, to the current that even we sense and feel? Dante wrote of "the love that moves the sun and the other stars." It is an objective love at the heart of creation. In our day, when humans are inflicting so much damage to life on earth, this petition brings to the fore the Father's love for all.

We grieve and suffer to see the good within anyone or anything we love thwarted or stifled or left fallow, or wither away from lack of proper nourishment. So must it grieve our Father when he looks on his creatures and his creation. Jesus teaches us to pray, "Thy will be done," to pray that nothing be wasted and all be fulfilled, "so that they may be one, as we are one" (John 17:11).

At the same time, to pray that the will of the Father be done is to acknowledge that it is not always accomplished and not always freely accepted. Freedom is our birthright as sons and daughters of God, and this inevitably means the freedom to go our own way, to turn away from the will of God and toward our own wills. We need look no further than ourselves for evidence of obstacles to the will of God, for brutishness, dullness, obstinacy; for a sense of being lost, in exile from the kingdom, remote from the Father's guiding influence.

WHAT IS UP TO US?

The religious traditions of the world agree in their analysis of the human condition. We could describe it ourselves—our plight is plain as day. This is how the Buddha portrayed it: "The mind is on fire, thoughts are on fire. . . . And with what are they on fire? With the fire of greed, with the fire of resentment, with the fire of infatuation." What the Buddha called "defilements:" envy, anger, enslavement to sensual pleasure, the desire for praise and honor, and all the rest, have been part of us, inextricably linked with human freedom, throughout the ages. That these same tendencies are called sins in the West does nothing to change their character or our experience of them. Turning to William Law, we hear an echo of the Buddha when he writes that in the "inmost ground of our soul" there is "a dark aching fire."

When quiet and still for a moment, each of us recognizes that something is amiss in the "inmost ground" of our soul. Despite all the talk of our free will, we know that we are "on fire," enslaved to the appetites and cravings of our hearts and minds and bodies. We are derailed by sin, one might well say, and very far from being able to obey the chief commandments of the Father: to love him, and our neighbors as ourselves. We are truly free only then, when our will and his are one.

When Christ has us pray "Thy will be done," our words reverberate far beyond our subjective dilemmas. We are asking God to bring about his redemptive plan both on earth and in heaven. One commentator notes that the request is not formulated that the will of God shall be executed by us, but that "*thy will shall come to pass* . . . as an event which takes place independently of our efforts." It is literally beyond us and our struggles, and yet as we call for the will of God to be done on earth as it is in heaven, we know it includes us. We cannot fail to hear the question being asked—Where are you? Where do you stand? Are you on the way, or are you a hindrance? What is the state of your will? Do you know? If not, how can you hope to be open to the will of God?

The will of God, operative and pervasive throughout time and eternity—as it was in the beginning, is now, and forever will be—nonetheless does not compel a single human being to conform to it. Thomas Aquinas wrote of this petition:

It must be noted that the very words . . . teach us a lesson. . . . It does not say, therefore, "Let us do," lest it would seem that the grace of God were left out; nor does it say, "Do," lest it would appear that our will and our zeal do not matter. He does say "Let it be done" through the grace of God, at the same time using our desire and our own efforts.

Without the grace of God we will never find our way to him. If we are passive, we are equally lost, for we close ourselves to the grace we need. It is not very clear perhaps, but even in our darkness we do recognize that something is up to us. We must cooperate. We must knock before the door is opened. And nothing can compel us to do so. We are free to shut ourselves off from the grace of God. At the same time we recall the "mere wish" that Gerard Manley Hopkins spoke of. Great effort is not required to begin; no heroic endeavor is asked for. The mere wish that we might do as God wishes, "might correspond, might say Yes to him," he says, is "our entire life and spirit." We will never comprehend the transcendent will of God, but if we are in touch with a wish within us to do as he wills, we have come before him. A habitual restricting and isolating attitude softens, and we become more malleable.

FROM DISARRAY TO ORDER

The Father seeks willing servants, and our liberty consists in that service alone. As we allow ourselves to enter more deeply into this petition, we experience a sense of submission. There is no struggle; we do not feel in any way opposed. We are aware of beginning to welcome a guiding authority, a healing influence. His will appears as a balm that soothes and quiets us. We are steadied in his gaze and, at the same time, sense that we are somehow being prepared.

This experience acts to upset our stubborn conviction—even if we think we know better—that to be free means to do as we like without impediment. We have been warned time and again that this is a fatal deception. We are free only to choose: either we are enslaved by our self-will, or we freely serve the will of God. Either we allow ourselves to be swept up into the selfish and self-destructive pursuits that enslave us, or we are disciples offering voluntary service. But this does not mean dividing ourselves into good and bad, into holy and ordinary. It does mean recognizing that our lives have a sacred dimension that could include and bring into context our stray and disordered impulses, impulses that do indeed "put obstacles in His way."

Discipline on behalf of the whole being is universally enjoined upon us. Thomas Merton reminds us that no one can live a decent life even on the most basic level if he is unable on occasion to refuse the impulses of his appetites:

No man who simply eats and drinks whenever he feels like eating and drinking, who smokes whenever he feels the urge to light a cigarette, who gratifies his curiosity and sensuality whenever they are stimulated, can consider himself a free person. He has renounced his spiritual freedom and become the servant of bodily impulse.

Therefore his mind and his will are not fully his own. They are under the power of his appetites.

Anyone who is trying to take time for the Lord's Prayer in the morning, for example, has first-hand knowledge of the inner tyrant Merton describes. Something doesn't want to stop, wants instead to be "free" to go about its business. Even when these objections are overcome and we take our seat in prayer, this "something" doesn't give up easily. It continues to assert its rights, insistently presenting its case for jumping up right now and answering the outer demands that it assures us simply can't wait. These impulses are impostors, pretending to speak for the whole. There are other, more insidious impulses—for power, for possessions, for prestige—that push themselves forward in our prayer and in our lives. They appear to be fighting on our behalf, but they are split off from the whole and very far from the will of the Creator. When we pray "on earth as it is in heaven," we pray that all be brought in order under the light and grace of God.

DIVINE LIBERTY

Maximos the Confessor wrote that the phrase "on earth as it is in heaven" refers to a place of stability established amid the ambitions and appetites that throw us off balance. This place of stability anchors "the whole power of the soul in divine and unassailable liberty." It is to this divine liberty that Christ refers when he says to his disciples, "Take my yoke upon you and learn from me; for I am gentle and humble in heart, and you will find rest for your souls" (Matthew 11:29).

This divine liberty *is* a yoke and a burden, but when we accept it willingly, we suddenly find "rest for our souls." It is not as though we must rid ourselves of ourselves in order to come to this rest. How could we do that? But it is possible to take off our blinders and open to a finer, more subtle current of life. To do God's will is to draw nearer to him. Dante wrote, "In his will is our peace," and in conformity to his will alone will we find rest—not a static cessation of movement but a vibrant and radiant fullness of being.

As we continue watching in prayer, another dimension slowly comes into view. Despite the chatter, restlessness, tension, and demands of all our impulses, the stillness of our bodies begins to alert us to a silence encompassing the current that habitually rushes outward. When we turn toward this stillness and silence, we are opening ourselves to grace. As we remain still, as we accept the yoke of stillness and silence, our outward-rushing impulses come under a yoke as well. We begin to see the necessity and desirability of prayer in a new way—in the moment. We are more fully present, more collected, more sane. We sense for ourselves that we are freer under this "yoke" than we were when we began to pray. No longer completely under the compulsions that usually drive us, we begin to approach what Maximos calls the "the divine and unassailable liberty."

This liberty is not the freedom to gratify impulses, but the freedom to be more transparent, less in the way. As our attentiveness grows, so does a new readiness to face the facts of our existence, to see everything as given. We are granted the help to see ourselves and all that takes place without judgment and granted also a measure of patience and humility. Helen Luke writes: "Whenever we accept a fact, accept with a will to rejoice, not just resigning ourselves to it, with all its causes in the past and all its potentialities in the future, then the seed is sown, the individual moves a tiny step toward consciousness, and so his will is done in earth and we have perhaps a glimpse of the unity 'as it is in Heaven,' of eternity and time as one thing."

As we pray "Thy will be done on earth as it is in heaven," we become aware that we live always in two currents: one in time, flowing outward; the other an eternal and inward streaming. We are not spiritual beings only, but incarnated on earth. We rightfully belong to both currents, but they are not both on the same level. When the lower, outer current dominates, we lose sight of the inner. When we surrender to the outward flow, we become lost and swallowed up in it. Not so the inner current: it can include the outer, allowing it to have its rightful place. We do not surrender to the inward flow by force—by directly attacking what seem to be distractions as we pray, for example—but by turning toward another life already active in us.

Efforts to reorder ourselves on our own terms and by our own devices in fact stimulate the very impulses we seek to suppress. Try as we might, our unruly nature cannot correct itself. "The only method to effect this," writes Kelpius, "is inward silence, by which the soul is turned wholly and altogether inward, to possess a present God." We need only turn willingly toward this grace to open ourselves to it. What seem impossible barriers melt away as our single-minded attachment to them fades. Our only "doing" is a simple turning of our attention. "A greater than ourselves is within us," counsels Benedictine Bede Frost. "Hinder Him not, do not contristate Him, and 'there is no need that any man should teach us.'" Our master is within and, when we wish to correspond, he guides us.

THE EMPTINESS OF FAITH AND LOVE

As we endeavor to listen to the Lord's Prayer, the stillness and silence glimpsed at one moment may disappear in the next. We may experience for a time what used to be called "sweetness" in prayer and then find ourselves completely lost, unsure of what we are doing and why, engulfed in doubt, our bearings lost. This is when we are tempted to give up, or grimly to stick with it, or to try to work up a feeling of devotion. At this moment, Paul advises us, "Do not be conformed to this world, but be transformed by the renewing of your minds, so that you may discern what is the will of God—what is good and acceptable and perfect" (Romans 12:2). At the moment of difficulty, "this world" would have us resort to our usual methods and take things into our own hands. The "renewing of our mind" will not come by succumbing to such suggestions. But what are we to do when for days or weeks we feel powerless and seemingly closed to grace, completely unable even to conceive of God's "good and acceptable and perfect" will?

Without exception, spiritual advisors have taught us to expect such periods in prayer, and further, to expect them to be more frequent and more difficult the longer one goes on. To persevere in prayer without "consolations" requires us to exercise our willingness in a way that would have otherwise eluded us. It leads us to see both the fruitlessness of struggle and our lack of trust in the Father. Renunciation and obedience, words that may have meant little before this struggle was accepted, take on real meaning. We are not good judges of our experience, we are told: what seem to us dry and pointless periods in prayer are in fact essential and active, clearing the way for the unexpected and unknown.

John of the Cross advises us that our will needs to be grounded in what he calls the "emptiness of faith and love," and not in a desire for spiritual experiences arising from our own subjective wishes. He points us toward a deep desire, one not based in emotionalism or sentimentality, but that instead carries us beyond our likes and dislikes. He enjoins upon us a mysterious emptiness, an "emptiness of faith and love," a pure intention that seeks not its own ends. Only from and within this emptiness can we truly pray "Thy will be done." Only then does this prayer evoke in us a wish to silently submit, and enable us to sense God's holy mystery and mercy.

A further experiment in listening to the Lord's Prayer can show us something of what is meant by this intentional fidelity in prayer. During each period devoted to the Lord's Prayer, quietly remain with a single phrase of the prayer. Refrain from saying the entire prayer; dwell with one phrase only. During one period dwell with the first phrase alone. During the next, the second, and so on. Allow the phrase to echo from time to time in the silence. If desired, include "Father" in the phrase, as in, "Father, hallowed be thy name;" "Father, thy kingdom come." Willingly accept this small restraint, and enter into the silence of God informed by his word. Listen in emptiness: do not wait for anything or expect anything. Attend to the phrase you are listening to. After going through the entire prayer in this way over seven periods of prayer, resume listening to the prayer as a whole. This phrase-by-phrase experiment may be undertaken from time to time as seems appropriate.

Trying this, we will experience a pressure to complete the prayer. Initially we will feel at odds with ourselves and somewhat at sea. We may complain, not see the point, or simply rebel. Two currents flicker in and out of view as we try to remain quietly meditating on the single phrase. We are drawn to the moment even as impulses arise to take us away. We do nothing and can do nothing to change the situation. We suffer these contrary currents, remembering to both watch and pray, remembering that we are not watching or praying alone, that the Father is always with us. We may at moments be brought back to Jesus' words, "Take my yoke upon you . . . and you will find rest for your souls," and find that a state of division and conflict is reconciled, and a space created where a new birth may come.

Christ said, "The Father and I are one," and we are reminded that in all he did and said he never acted or spoke alone. While on earth, as in heaven, he was always with the Father, and he calls us to this union with the Father and with one another. As Christ bore the earthly, he enables us to bear the heavenly.

We have reached the midpoint of the prayer. It is a moment of dwelling deeply within the will of the Father, of renewal and remembrance of God's desire that we draw near to him. We will go on to express our needs and fears, to confess our sins, and to forgive and beg forgiveness, but here we are invited to be at rest in "the divine and unassailable liberty." That we be led to this liberty and be established in it we pray, "Thy will be done."

CHAPTER 7

Give us this day our daily bread:

Essential Hunger

With the words "on earth as it is in heaven" we reached the mid-point of the Lord's Prayer. These words are like the hinge upon which a gate swings, opening to one side and another; like the hinge upon which the breath swings in its movement in and out again. "On earth as it is in heaven" refers to each of the first three petitions—the in-breath of the prayer—and also is prologue to the next three the out-breath of the prayer. The prayer is said to contain the whole of the gospel in brief, and during the in-breath of its cycle of respiration we are indirectly and gradually, perhaps, but very certainly initiated into the great glories of the Christian way: faith, hope, and love.

References to "these three" appear again and again in the King James Version of the New Testament, and the Lord's Prayer orients us toward faith, hope, and love the very moment the prayer opens and we turn toward the Father. "Hallowed be thy name," and we are shown the glory of the living God. It is a glory far beyond the reach of reason, a glory that awakens a faith in us that is part of our very being. Faith, hope, and love, we see, are not acts but attributes—part of our human nature. When Christ calls us to new life, he is calling us to these lights hidden within. In the Lord's Prayer he is awakening us to our nature and destiny. At the outset we are invited, in the Psalmist's words, to "enter into his gates with thanksgiving and into his courts with praise," to be thankful and bless his name. He means to establish and steady us in this essential faith, and to recall to us that here and nowhere else is where we find our rest.

"Thy kingdom come," and the substance of hope appears, not a hope *for* something but the experience of hope fulfilled: we are brought into a present kingdom, and before a present God.

"Thy will be done," and we are enlightened, brought into communion, flooded in the infinite light of love. Faith, hope, and love; Father, Son, and Holy Spirit: "these three."

Neither faith nor hope nor love can be fed and strengthened in us as the prayer intends unless we heed Christ's words to pray "not as the heathens do." He tells us to go into our room, to shut the door, and to pray in secret. Christ gives us these conditions so that the Father will be able to come to us with his gifts of faith and hope and love. Unless we withdraw from the crowd—both in the streets and within our hearts and minds—we may have a reward, but it will not be what the Father is waiting to give.

Often we find ourselves with one foot in the street and one in our room, unable to close the door, the clamor of the crowd still echoing. Christ calls us to enter into a secret place, a place that is dark to our usual way of being. He asks us to still our ambitions, to quiet our anxieties, to trust in the Father through him. For this we must take leave of what we usually rely upon. Our reason, our imagination, our beliefs all fall far short of the reality of the living God. Meister Eckhart long ago wrote that all we can think or say about God is untrue. Christ tells us we must enter with him into what is obscure to us. Only then, in this secret place, when the door is closed, can the source of faith, the substance of hope, the light of love come to us.

A prayer to the Holy Spirit beloved by Orthodox Christians can help us find our way to this secret place, can help the inward turning. Say it, if you wish, quietly and calmly, after watching the breathing for a time just before beginning the Lord's Prayer:

> O Heavenly King,
> O Comforter,
> The Spirit of truth, who art everywhere
> and fillest all things,
> treasure of blessings, and giver of life, come,
> and abide in us.

Cleanse us of our impurities,
and of thy goodness, save our souls. Amen

This prayer to the Holy Spirit prepares us to begin the Lord's Prayer in what John of the Cross called the "emptiness of faith and love," naked before God, empty of sentimentality, ambition, doubt, and fear. It reveals the secret place within as spacious and expansive. We are not confined in our closet but liberated.

DRAWING NEARER TO EACH OTHER

What we have called the in-breath of the Lord's Prayer fills us with the Spirit. "Give us this day . . . ," we pray, and the out-breath of the prayer begins. Imbued with the grace of the Spirit, and in the light of the kingdom and will of God, we make our petitions—for bread, for forgiveness, for protection. We have been prepared to ask for our earthly needs in light of the heavenly. And the first thing we are taught to ask for is our daily bread.

As we begin the out-breath of the prayer, we become aware that the time of prayer in the secret place will come to an end. We will again be on the street corners, in the marketplace, amid the noise and pulls of life on earth. We know we have been lost in forgetfulness before, and will forget again. Help us to remember, we pray; give us the bread of remembrance. Strengthen in us the remembrance of you; of your love for us, the love you would have us share with each other.

In the sixth century Abba Dorotheus asked us to imagine a circle with rays going out from its center. As we move inward, wishing to draw nearer to God, we at the same time draw nearer to each other. When we turn toward external things and withdraw from the central point, in the same degree we withdraw from each other. During the Lord's Prayer we have been fed, and soon we will be hungry for God and for the certainty of communion with others. In the midst of outer demands we pray: Grant us the grace to remember you and to turn toward you as we have been led to do during the time of prayer.

Our request for bread is a declaration of our common need, and it is only when we recognize this need that we are joined in community. "We meet the incarnate Word of God in the other human being because God himself really is in this other," writes German theologian Karl Rahner. "If we love him, if we do not as it were culpably impede the dynamism of this love and fundamentally turn it back upon ourselves, there occurs precisely the divine descent into the flesh of man, so that God is in the place where we are and gazes at us in a human being." When we recognize our common Father—and our common struggle to awaken to him—our life among others need not fling us far from the center, but can instead prompt an inward turn and awaken us from our trance of self-absorption. It is in this recognition we are able to honor and serve others with humility, empty of egoism.

A disciple asked Jesus to teach us to pray, and Jesus responded to him and to us as disciples. Would any disciple of Christ have asked, "Teach *me* to pray"? Would he have approached his master asking for a special instruction, a unique method, just for him? No, he asks for a prayer in common, a prayer for all. And Christ, after summoning us before the Father's glory, his kingdom, and his will, bids us ask for that which will sustains us as sons and daughters of the Father, as members of the body of Christ, as brothers and sisters. Christ tells us the kingdom is within us, among us. It is here, now, and coming in its fullness. He knows that our essential hunger and primary need at every moment is for bread to nourish our new life in common, our shared life in Christ.

THE BREAD OF HEAVEN

In this petition is a Greek word that appears only twice in the Greek New Testament, only in the Luke and Matthew versions of the Lord's Prayer. The word is *epiousion*. Though it is usually translated as "daily," scholars have long disputed its exact meaning, some proposing "tomorrow's" or "the coming day's." As we listen to the Lord's Prayer, we sense that Jeremias' research into Jesus' Aramaic has uncovered what the prayer intends: what we are asking for is the bread of tomorrow in the sense of the bread of the coming age. This is the bread of heaven, the bread of life. Of this bread and no other we stand in need at every moment. "Today, Lord," wrote Bonaventure in the thirteenth century, "give us this bread, so that we have it present and keep it ever present. . . . May this bread be ever present . . . and never may it be only past or future."

We ask for this bread "today," and have been told that when we ask, it will be given. Do we see the necessity of it? Do we think that we can get by with earthly bread alone, and that this bread of life is something extra? As we listen to the Lord's Prayer we are shown that this can never be so. A human life touches both the eternal and the temporal, or it is no longer human. An earthly life alone is in fact subhuman. Christ teaches that it is imperative to ask for this bread every day, to realize we cannot go a single day without it. Otherwise, our egoistic impulses, unregarded and unattended, will soon engulf us. Only in watching and praying does the whole human being appear, body, soul, mind, heart, and spirit.

Seventeenth-century English mystic John Flavel writes of Proverbs 4:23, "Keep your heart with all vigilance; for from it flow the springs of life," that it calls us to a constant renewal of attention, moment by moment:

> Even a gracious heart is like a musical instrument, which though it be exactly tuned, a small matter brings it out of tune again; yea, hang it aside but a little, and it will need setting again. . . . If gracious hearts are in a desirable frame in one duty, yet how dull, dead, and disordered when they come to another! Therefore every act requires a particular preparation of the heart.

We are led to moments of presence and balance in the Lord's Prayer, and when we pray for our daily bread we are praying to remember this state of being attuned—and the way toward it. Listening to the prayer is like a laboratory or master class that prepares us for exactly the same effort of attention and of return that is enjoined upon us when the prayer ends. Coming in and out of tune, approaching and falling away, occurs again and again during the Lord's Prayer: it is through this process that it teaches us the "particular preparation of the heart" needed amid the conditions both of prayer and of our everyday life. When we pray for bread we pray that we may come to this state of being attuned within the time of prayer and when the prayer is over. Without it we forget. We become lukewarm, then indifferent, and finally lost. And we are unanimously counseled to pray daily—not to miss a single day—whether we are satisfied by our prayer or not, whether it seems profitable or not, whether is a success or not, even if it is uncongenial or seems pointless. We are faithful and patient, acknowledging our helplessness. Whether or not it seems so to us, each daily encounter nourishes the next.

"Do this in memory of me," Christ said as he broke bread at the Last Supper. Christ is the host not only at the eucharistic feast, but in all sharing of bread and work, all mutual support and affection. As we ask for our daily bread we pray that by its grace every moment, every encounter, every act may be sanctified, may be lived in the liberty of the spirit and not in the slavery of division and estrangement.

SEEK FIRST THE KINGDOM

In the Gospels Jesus is often at table with his disciples, and even prepares an early breakfast for them by the shore. He is aware of the needs of our earthly life and never disregards them. Nor do we disregard the need so many have for physical bread each day. We who do not suffer physical hunger cannot but be aware of those who do. They appear before us at this point in our prayer. The entreaty for the bread of tomorrow, the bread of heaven, "does not sever everyday life and the kingdom of God from one another," says Jeremias, "but it encompasses the totality of life. It embraces everything that Jesus' disciples need for body and soul. It includes 'daily bread,' but it does not content itself with that. It asks that amid the secularity of everyday life the powers and gifts of God's coming age might be active in all that Jesus' disciples do in word and deed . . . even now, even here, today."

Immediately before the Lord's Prayer in Matthew Jesus assures us that "your Father knows what you need before you ask him," and later in the chapter, just after the prayer, speaks to us at length about our worries. He knows them in detail. Don't worry, he tells us, your Father knows you need all these things. Don't waste your life on such worries—all your worrying will not add a single moment to the span of your lives. Especially do not worry about tomorrow, he says knowingly—"today's trouble is enough for today."

He tells us what we are to do: "Strive first for the kingdom of God and his righteousness, and all these things will be given to you as well" (Matthew 6:33). He doesn't say we do not need food or clothing, but that they will come in addition, when we seek first things first, when we attend to what is before us "this day" and give ourselves fully to each encounter, each demand, the smallest act.

But in this is our entire dilemma: we cannot cease worrying until we seek the kingdom, and we cannot strive for the kingdom while we are engulfed in worries. Unless we seek it first in our lives it will not be first in our lives, and we know it is impossible to come to this on our own. Our tendency is to run away or to give up in the face of our powerlessness, but to experience our inability is exactly what we need. When we accept this burden of powerlessness, when we shoulder it, it is the lightest thing in the world. Only when we see our weakness, when we witness all our fears and uncertainties, do we earnestly pray, "Give us this day our daily bread." Let us hunger for this bread. Let us receive it, let us share it, and let it not be past or future, but ever present: "For everyone who asks receives, and everyone who searches finds, and for everyone who knocks, the door will be opened" (Matthew 7:8).

Christ tells us not to worry about tomorrow, but he also counsels us not to put off till tomorrow our search for the kingdom. Seek it first, seek it now, he says. He shepherds us out of the unreality of our imaginary anxieties and into the reality of the present moment. He is always and only in the present, now, and it is in the present alone that we can hear his voice and receive our daily bread.

Among the Spiritual Exercises of Ignatius of Loyola is one that helps bring us into the present. This is a method of prayer, as Ignatius says, "by rhythm." It is linked with the breathing: with each breath one says a word of the Lord's Prayer so that "only one word be said between one breath and another." There is to be no alteration of the breathing, no tension. It is advisable to watch and listen for the space of a few breaths between each phrase of the prayer. Attend in silence, staying with the breathing and with the awareness of the whole body present in this listening. When the prayer is finished, remain a few moments longer, "keeping the heart."

CHAPTER 8

And forgive us our debts as we also have forgiven our debtors:

Entering the Present

nd forgive us . . . As we listen to the prayer we hear this petition following upon the need for daily bread. We ask to be fed on the bread of another level of life *and*, thus nourished, to receive forgiveness and the grace to forgive at the same moment. The outward breath of the prayer, flowing on, ends with a plea to the Father to preserve us in the wholeness and reconciliation in which he has established us.

Rarely is the experience of the Lord's Prayer fully realized, however, and perhaps nowhere in the prayer are we so often troubled as we are here. Each time you come to this phrase, watch anew. Do you approach this expression of your deepest need with a sense of freedom and release? Does it come instead as a judge, reminding you of your failings and reawakening stubborn resentments? Do you feel somewhat in the dark about your standing before God and others? Is your need for forgiveness present to you? Are anger and bitterness far more vivid than your failings? Or are you rather dull and impassive, taking your own forgiveness for granted and sliding over your inability to forgive?

Somewhere we know that on our own it is no more possible for us to forgive than it is for us not to worry about tomorrow. As if behind a screen, our mistakes, regrets, hurt pride, insults inflicted and received, offenses, injuries, guilts, and betrayals swarm. Better move on than become entangled there!

We read of those in centuries past who, knowing of their inability to forgive, would omit these words, but such evasion cannot succeed. Forgiveness is in the present moment, but it encompasses our past: our history clings to us, and we to it. To see this history, and to recognize it as a barrier, is at the heart of this petition, for only when touched by mercy do we see how deeply this barrier is entrenched in us. Until then we are unaware of it, and consequently little concerned. We pray for forgiveness—for the grace and mercy to know even for a moment what it means to have this barrier fall away. We pray that we may feel remorse for our blindness and egotism and know that the walls that keep us from knowing the Father's mercy are made of the same stones as those that prevent us from being at peace with others.

What needs forgiveness and forgiving, we see, is tied to the past, to the history of *me,* the partial self we iden- tify with, the small egotism that takes all our attention and is always insisting on its rights. Everything that belongs to *me* is there, jealously guarded. That's why the word *us* in the Lord's Prayer can rankle. We feel quite proprietary about our past: *I* am the one who has been wronged, overlooked, unjustly accused, unrewarded, after all. What has anyone else to do with it? And how can anyone share my blame, it asks? It is *I* who miss the mark, *I* who have debts, *I* who run roughshod over others: *my* sins are unique to *me* and *I* am the one who needs forgiveness. What has this to do with others? the same voice peevishly complains. We see that it is not only to our anger and resentment that we cling so tenaciously, but also to our suffering. This suffering is ours alone, it distinguishes us from others, and we don't want to relinquish it. It is from this morass of our egotism; from our guilt, false and real; from all our grasping and clinging to *me* that Christ frees us in this petition of the Lord's Prayer.

SUFFERING OUR REFUSAL TO FORGIVE

When led by grace to be wholly present for even a moment to this petition, this past is annihilated. When open to the mercy of forgiveness, the links of the chain that bind past to future are broken. In the light of the Father's forgiveness, we are reconciled and loosed from the deadly grasp of recrimination.

At that moment the past is powerless—no longer capable of casting its consequences forward to spoil our future. In forgiveness and forgiving we are liberated. No longer bound to our history, we are freed to relate to the present moment, open to the will of the Father and his kingdom. Is this not what it means to be saved?

Near death we would pray with clarity and understanding, "Forgive us our trespasses as we forgive those who trespass against us." What seemed important in the midst of life—prestige, power, honor, possessions—would fade to nothing. At the point of death we would know from what we need to be freed and cleansed, what we would pray fall away from us. Whenever we enter this petition truly, we willingly die to our self-assertion, our self-reliance, all our prior claims: we are given the grace to die to ourselves for a moment; to die to that *me* that is usually in control. Our demands on God and others cease. Simone Weil writes:

> At the moment of saying these words we must have already remitted everything that is owing to us. This not only includes reparation for any wrongs we think we have suffered, but also gratitude for the good we think we have done, and it applies in a quite general way to all we expect from people and things, to all we consider as our due and without which we should feel ourselves to have been frustrated. All these are the rights that we think the past has given us over the future.

But often these claims persist. We feel incapable of forgiving or knowing forgiveness. We cannot *do* either, but can suffer our condition: praying, we can keep watch. Thus far in the prayer all has flowed from the Father, but this petition asks something of us: even God himself cannot open our clenched fist. As we are forgiven, so must we forgive, Christ tells us, but we *cannot* forgive, and the grace of forgiveness cannot reach us. Rather than decreasing the tension, at this point in the prayer, make a change in your exercise and allow the tension to increase. To the phrase "forgive us our trespasses," listen as usual in silence. At the phrase "as we forgive those who trespass against us," allow to rise up those persons, incidents, or events you are reluctant to forgive. Allow them to show themselves in the quiet. Without self-justification or defensiveness, see and suffer your inability to forgive.

The need for forgiveness and forgiving usually is concealed and buried out of sight. Novelist Flannery O'Connor tells in a short story of a moment when this need was revealed:

> Mr. Head had never known before what mercy felt like because he had been too good to deserve any, but he felt he knew now. . . .
>
> He stood very still and felt the action of mercy touch him again but this time he knew that there were no words in the world that could name it. He understood that it grew out of agony, which is not denied to any man and which is given in strange ways to children. He understood it was all a man could carry into death to give his Maker and he suddenly burned with shame that he had so little of

it to take with him. He stood appalled, judging himself with the thoroughness of God, while the action of mercy covered his pride like a flame and consumed it. He had never thought himself a great sinner before but he saw now that his true depravity had been hidden from him lest it cause him despair. He realized that he was forgiven for sins from the beginning of time, when he had conceived in his own heart the sin of Adam, until the present, when he had denied poor Nelson. He saw that no sin was too monstrous for him to claim as his own, and since God loved in proportion as He forgave, he felt ready at that instant to enter Paradise.

Flannery's Mr. Head knows himself, sees himself. He is in the present moment and does not turn away. He does not attempt to escape into reaction: into guilt, or despair, or denial. He stays. He stays in the present moment, and the Lord is with him. In gratitude he feels his smugness, complacency, and self-righteousness fall away; he receives mercy, and he himself is capable of mercy to others.

Mr. Head's experience reveals to us again that each phrase of the Lord's Prayer contains all the rest, each reflecting and encompassing a holographic unity. Mr. Head prays for mercy to the Father, and the Father's glory is made manifest; his will is done; his kingdom comes; he gives him his daily bread; and he forgives him, as he forgives others.

AN AWAKENING FORCE

We have two translations of this petition, one speaking of trespass, another of debt. They are both summed up in Paul's observation that "I do not do the good I want, but the evil I do not want is what I do" (Romans 7:19). We offend and injure others both by omission and commission: by withholding what should not be withheld and by doing what should not be done. This petition to forgive and be forgiven, intensely experienced within the prayer, will soon operate in our lives outside the time of prayer. We begin to watch how often trespass and debt mingle in our encounters with others. Are we callous when caring is vital, cold when warmth is called for, heedless when our attention is needed? We watch for the tyranny of *me* committing trespass, incurring debt. Seeing our solicitous care for ourselves, we slowly become more aware of the feelings of others. Do we respect their integrity and independence? Do we recognize their essential freedom? Do we instead insist they adopt our opinions? Are we eager to "put them on the right road"? Are we determined to give advice and resentful when it is not taken? The prayer brings questions such as these alive within us and leads us back to a larger presence of which this *me* is only a part, and no longer speaks for the whole.

While we are on the alert for our own offenses, Louis Evely reminds us to pause and remember to forgive a particular someone who "has disappointed and offended us, someone with whom we are continually displeased and with whom we are more spiteful than we

would dare be with anyone else. That is ourselves. . . .
We would never dare judge any other of God's creatures
with the contemptuous negligence with which we
crush ourselves." If we are to love others as ourselves,
this inner discord and antipathy must first be extin-
guished in God's mercy. We cannot compel mercy but
we can know our need, and know it as the need we
share with all others.

To love God with our whole heart, soul, and mind,
Christ says, is the greatest commandment; and the
second is like it: to love our neighbor as ourselves. He
has bid us love as we are loved, to forgive as we are
forgiven, and to know our shared life in him and in the
Father. This loving and knowing will not come once
and for all but must be ever-renewed. What is needed
to see that at every moment we follow either our
personal will or the will of God, that at every moment
we choose either the way to death and darkness or the
way to life and light?

A spiritual teacher of the last century says that
remembering our death while in the midst of life is a
potent force for this awakening. He urges each one to
"constantly sense and be aware of the inevitability of
his own death, as well as of the death of everyone
upon whom his eyes, or attention rests." This is difficult,
seemingly impossible, but if we persist in trying to
come to this awareness the little *me* becomes sober,
narcissism and illusions fade, a more real world
appears, and the taste for revenge and presumption
subsides. We feel anew the need to pray, "Forgive us
our debts as we also have forgiven our debtors."

Perhaps then we can begin to wish, as Paul advocates in Romans 15, to "please our neighbor for the good purpose of building up the neighbor." "May the God of steadfastness and encouragement grant you to live in harmony with one another, in accordance with Christ Jesus," he concludes, "so that together you may with one voice glorify the God and Father of our Lord Jesus Christ."

CHAPTER 9

And lead us not into temptation, but deliver us from evil:

Strength in the Struggle

In the midst of the glories and mercies of the Lord's Prayer come these disturbing and confounding words. They are the last in the prayer, a cry for protection and rescue, but do we feel in distress? They refer to temptation to sin, surely, but while long lists of sins come to mind, do any seem a matter of life and death? Unworthy impulses and acts, none alien, but as we listen in the prayer do we have a sense of danger? Does evil, the fruit of temptation, come before us as a present menace and a peril? We pray only for the essential in the Lord's Prayer, and temptation as an essential threat escapes us. This meaning of temptation we cannot find, and the phrase of the prayer rings false. It is an appeal for help, and not to feel in need of this help is troubling. What is eluding us?

As we have seen, the prayer is the greatest teacher of the Christian Way, and as we search more earnestly it will reveal to us the nature of this threat.

Let's begin, with George MacDonald, at the beginning:

> I hope you don't think God made us, and made the world, out of nothing. I don't believe God made anything out of nothing; I think He made all things out of Himself. And making us thus out of Himself, the problem was how to make us so that we should be ourselves; and so I sometimes think He took a great trouble *to throw us off, as it were, so far out of Himself as that we might become ourselves*, and develop a will and a free will of our own, and with that free will turn around and seek Him.

God made us free so that we might seek him . . . and also, being free, might not. We might instead forget, and decide that our selves and what we see around us are all that need concern us. Granted independence and the freedom to "turn around and seek Him," we are equally free to fall instead under influences that enslave us. This slavery feels like empowerment, and we like it. To rely on our own strength, to wish to have this power increased unto total self-sufficiency, is also part of our nature. James 1:13-14 makes it quite clear that God tempts no one, that each of us is tempted when lured and enticed by our own desire.

We have seen that the Lord's Prayer is a laboratory for watching and praying, and here, at this petition, the connotation of being on guard comes to the fore. But, again, for what exactly are we to be on guard?

Turning again to the Lord's Prayer, we see that it is a teacher indeed. Let us invert the prayer, change its direction, and see what it reveals. Instead of "Our Father . . . hallowed by thy name," let us say:

> Master of Earth,
> Exalt my name over all others.
> Give me a kingdom where my will is never thwarted.
> Let me take whatever I wish, and grant me vengeance over all who oppose me.
> Let me satisfy my every desire,
> And give me the power to crush anyone who stands in my way.

Even in this cynical age, the inversion shocks. It is an infernal prayer, and we know it as coming straight from hell even if we aren't quite sure we believe in such a place. Lived daily, it will surely lead us to the realm of the damned. But it allows us to see how the Lord's Prayer, subtly and indirectly, reveals our gravest temptation, the temptation to usurp divine authority and to set ourselves up as little gods. Phrase by phrase the prayer overthrows this little god, corrects us, and guides us. The Lord's Prayer protects us from the infernal prayer that tempts all of us, always, at every moment. The prayer teaches us to discern whether we are under the tyranny of the "little me," bound by its egocentric perspective, or opening to the kingdom of shared being.

In the Lord's Prayer, Christ has granted us an antidote and a remedy. Each phrase reorients us, alerts us, reminds us, and sets us in order again. It helps us to know that it is to his name, his kingdom, and his will we are called to turn in liberty and joy and that to turn to ourselves is perdition.

Phrase by phrase the prayer shows us how limited is our vision and how terrible the grip of our habitual selfishness. As the light of conscience grows brighter, we see ourselves as we are and begin to suffer. Our heart of stone starts to soften. We begin to know that this remorse is not something we do, but is itself a gift. Our awakened conscience makes room for the warmth and radiance of the Holy Spirit to act within us.

Within the spaciousness of the prayer, a new possibility opens for us. We enter an expanse where, as French theologian Yves Congar says, "we cry Abba! Father! But we say this through the Spirit. . . . He has been sent 'into our hearts' and, as the Holy Spirit, he is so pure, subtle and penetrating that he is able to be in all of us and in each one of us without doing violence to the person, indiscernible in his spontaneous movement. He is above all the Spirit of freedom."

What we have seen of the double meaning of each phrase of the prayer holds here as well. Conscience is a divine gift of the Spirit, but something is up to us. Conscience grants us the capacity to know ourselves, but we must assent to this knowledge. Every moment invites us to awaken to influences and impulses that could be our daily bread. On one side, consciously alert to the choices before us; on the other, opening to the influence of the Father: watching and praying, our whole being is nourished and renewed. We then become more truly ourselves, more consciously bearing the wish to have "a free will of our own, and with that free will turn around and seek Him."

Choice made in the light of an awakened conscience is implicit in all the petitions, but here it is made plain that this choice is the crux of our lives. In this light, our prayer becomes urgent. We pray to be spared from choices that imprison us in the citadel of our selfishness, and to be delivered from the evil harvest of those choices that come from and are made on behalf of the little *me* alone.

STRUGGLE AND SELF-KNOWLEDGE

In his writing on the Lord's Prayer, Martin Luther speaks of the evils that "cleave to us by nature," and those "to which we are incited by the society, example, and what we hear and see of other people," and those that come from "the world, which offends us in word and deed, and impels us to anger and impatience"; a world wherein "there is nothing but hatred and envy, enmity, violence and wrong, unfaithfulness, vengeance, cursing, raillery, slander, pride and haughtiness, with superfluous finery, honor, fame and power, where no one is willing to be the least, but every one desires to sit at the head and to be seen before all." All these evils, he says, "wound and inflame even the innocent heart."

Clearly Luther is writing of inescapable forces, and not all of them self-generated. These too, circumscribe us, though they are not manifestations of a perverse free will. Indeed in these descriptions the question of our free will seems moot. But if we are not aware of the movements of our mind and desires—whatever compels them—if we cannot see these movements from a consciousness that witnesses in freedom, then we are simply driven by reaction to inner and outer events. Without detachment from our actions and the desires that drive them we suffer, but our suffering is partial and oppresses us. We feel victimized, and are deprived of the vision that enables liberating sacrifice on behalf of a greater whole.

Whether we consciously or unconsciously cooperate with the processes that enslave us, we cannot escape the consequences of our thoughts and actions. The Desert Fathers offer very precise descriptions of what happens when—in the absence of inner vigilance and discernment—an initially harmless impression invades us and captures our attention. Russian Orthodox theologian Paul Evdokimov summarizes the teaching of the Desert Fathers about this process and about why it is so important to "strike the serpent on the head":

> Something very fleeting arises abruptly and solicits our attention. From the subconscious the appeal rises to consciousness and makes an effort to be kept

there. This is not yet sin, far from it, but it is the presence of a suggestion. It is in this first moment that the immediate reaction of one's attention is decisive. The temptation is going to leave or remain. The spiritual masters make use of an image that was familiar in the desert: "Strike the serpent on the head" before he enters the cell. If the serpent enters, the struggle will be much more laborious.

How many times have we caught a glimpse of the entering serpent? We willingly and with pleasure begin to entertain a devious or deceitful or spiteful thought that had no particular force at its first appearance. It needs to be fed to grow, and we feed it. To "deliver us from evil" translated literally is not a plea to be liberated but to be snatched from the jaws of evil. It is a prayer for immediate rescue from despair and apostasy. Again we have a part to play—to see our seduction and nip it in the bud. Evdokimov continues:

> If our attention does not react, the following phase is indulgence. A willing attentiveness to the tempting solicitation causes a certain pleasure, becoming an equivocal attitude that is already cooperating. St. Ephrem speaks of the "pleasant conversation" of the soul with a persistent suggestion.
>
> An enjoyment by anticipation, imaginary at the moment, marks the third stage. A tacit agreement, an unavowed consent, orients one toward an accomplishment deemed possible, for it is passionately desirable. Theoretically, the decision has indeed been made. In coveting the object, the sin has been

mentally committed. This is the judgment of the Gospel on the impure gaze in which adultery has already been pre-consummated.

The fourth stage effectively consummates the act. It forms the beginning of a passion, of a thirst henceforth unquenchable. When it has become a habit, the passion neutralizes every resistance. The person disintegrates in powerlessness. Bewitched, he leans toward his implacable end: despair, fearful *accedia,* disgust or anxiety, madness or suicide, in all cases, spiritual death.

When we reach this petition, we have already been told to ask for our daily bread—bread for the struggle that engages us at every moment. We cannot escape this struggle, and we are asked to seek help amid what is certain and unavoidable. The capacity to be tempted is necessary to the Christian process of self-knowledge, to the process of death and rebirth that the prayer activates and awakens within us. Temptation itself is inescapable; no one is free of it. We are responsible not for its presence in us, but to watch and pray that the unavoidable triumphalism of the unenlightened ego be seen and neutralized by sacrifice and suffering. We watch and pray to comprehend the greater whole that is in question with every breath. Are we moving toward or away from awareness of the spiritual reality within us?

As we go on listening to the Lord's Prayer, discernment in regard to this movement toward or away from the essential is sharpened and strengthened. We discover more and more subtle levels of the reaching and resisting spoken of earlier. At each moment, listening to the prayer puts us in question: a moment comes when we are quieter and more receptive than usual; the mind formulates a thought congratulating us, and the equilibrium that was establishing itself within us is gone. We recognize the intrusion of this thought, see that it reduces us to a spectator rather than a participant in the prayer, and begin again. The difference between what was granting us an entry into another level of life and what blocked that entry becomes minutely but definitely clearer. We discern that the impulses come from two different sources, one active and vivifying, the other passive and deadening. The wish to be available to the one and not seduced by the other grows. Jeremias notes that the meaning of this last petition does not reference "preservation *from* temptation but preservation *in* temptation"—we pray not to be spared but strengthened.

For example, when we approach the prayer again after a deep experience of it, we may notice that a part of us is expecting the experience to repeat itself. Perhaps something feels that it has finally learned how to "do" the prayer and comes to the next encounter confident and a bit self-satisfied. This confidence is soon lost in a gloomy fog of confusion. We don't know what happened or what we are doing wrong. As this happens again and again, we begin to see that we are fogged in because our trust has shifted: we have come to prayer relying on our own abilities. In so doing, we have closed ourselves to what is being offered to us, and offered again. Listening to the prayer undermines our reliance on what is unreliable and orients us more deeply within.

Teresa of Avila noted in her writings about the Lord's Prayer that "if we try to grasp we will lose all." Inevitably, we *will* try to grasp, and *will* lose all. We may arrive at a period when we feel desolate and empty, and the prayer seems devoid of meaning. If we don't discern that it was the demand for "results" that led to our isolation, our discouragement may grow into despair. Finally we may stop altogether, giving up on both ourselves and prayer. We shall have allowed ourselves to be led into temptation. We shall have come to the test and not seen it as a test but simply have been swallowed up, and it may be a long time before we feel the need to pray again.

When temptation comes Jesus teaches us to pray in the midst of it: be with us, call us back to you, direct our gaze to you, and turn us away from dependence on our reason and its judgments, from our demands, from division and spiritual death.

That temptation must come is corroborated by an ancient saying that, Jeremias notes, Jesus "spoke on the last evening, prior to the prayer in Gethsemane: 'No one can obtain the kingdom of heaven who has not passed through temptation.'" This passing through temptation is ceaseless; that is why our watching and praying must also be ceaseless and never finished once and for all.

AN EVER-PRESENT DANGER

It will help us here to remember in what contexts Christ spoke the words "Watch and pray." During his agony in Gethsemane near the end of his own life on earth, he finds his disciples sleeping and asks, "What, could ye not watch with me one hour? Watch and pray, that ye enter not into temptation: the spirit indeed is willing, but the flesh is weak" (Matthew 26:40-41 KJV). And when he is describing the signs of the end, the last days, he says, "Take ye heed, watch and pray: for ye know not when the time is. For the Son of Man is as a man taking a far journey, who left his house, and gave authority to his servants, and to every man his work, and commandeth the porter to watch. Watch ye therefore: for ye know not when the master of the house cometh, at even, or at midnight, or at the cock-crowing, or in the morning: Lest coming suddenly he find you sleeping. And what I say unto you I say unto all, Watch" (Mark 13:33–37 KJV).

"Against this background of darkest portent," writes theologian Heinz Schürmann,

> Jesus' exhortation to pray for deliverance from temptation takes on a new and deeper meaning. . . . It springs from the arena of Christ's combat with the devil which will attain its peak of intensity at the end of the world. . . . Yet Christ never tells us to pray that God will spare us from undergoing these great trials. He knows that the coming of the kingdom must be preceded by decisive conflict, and indeed, must result from it. Even now has arrived

the "day," the "hour," the very "moment" of our temptation; so that our situation is basically the same as that which will prevail at the end of time.

"Our situation is the same": as we are tempted now, so we are at the hour of our death and at the end of time. This phrase of the prayer has taken us from the trials of our everyday lives to the trials of the last days attendant upon the coming of the kingdom. The last petition of the Lord's Prayer is the cry of those who know the danger besetting them at every moment is the same as on the last day: the danger of falling away from God. Now and always our need is one and the source of all strength and help is one. In the name of him in whom all time is gathered up we pray, "Lead us not into temptation, but deliver us from evil." Amen.

CHAPTER 10

Evocations

B*efore teaching us the Lord's Prayer, Christ said, "After this manner therefore pray ye" and from the Middle Ages onward there has been a tradition of paraphrase of the prayer, each effort revealing its living spirit. Examples beginning with Francis of Assisi in the twelfth century and Dante in the fourteenth are followed here by reflections on the prayer from contemporary Christians, responses to a call for a renewal of this tradition in our own day. It is hoped that readers will attempt their own written meditation on the prayer, recording for themselves the fruit of their listening.*

1. FRANCIS OF ASSISI

Our Father, our most blessed, most holy Creator, our Savior and our Comforter; who art in heaven, in the angels, in the saints, enlightening them to know Thee; because Thou, O Lord, art the light that inflames them by Thy divine love; because Thou, O Lord, art the love which is in them and fills them to render them blessed; because Thou, O Lord, art the highest good, and the eternal good, from which all good things come, and without which there is no good anywhere.

Hallowed be Thy name: let the knowledge of Thee become apparent to us, so that we may know how plentiful are Thy blessings, how long Thy promises, how lofty Thy majesty, how profound Thy judgments.

Thy Kingdom come; that Thou shouldst reign within us with Thy grace and let us come to Thy Kingdom, where we will see Thee face to face, and have perfect love, blessed company, and sempiternal joy.

Thy will be done on earth as it is in heaven; so that we may love Thee with all our heart, thinking ever of Thee; with all our soul, ever desiring Thee; with all our mind, directing all our intentions to Thee, and seeking Thy honor in all things; and with all our strength, employing all the power of our spirit and all the senses of our body in the service of Thy love, and in naught else: and that we may also love our neighbors as ourselves, drawing all men, as far as it is in our power, toward Thy love, rejoicing in the good things of others and grieving at their ills as at our own, and never giving offense to anyone.

Give us this day our daily bread, that is Thy beloved Son, our Lord Jesus Christ, in memory of the love he bore us, and of what he said, did, and suffered for us.

And forgive us our trespasses as we forgive those who trespass against us; and what we do not forgive entirely, make Thou, O Lord, that we should forgive, so that for Thy sake we should sincerely love our enemies, and intercede devoutly for them with Thee, and never render evil for evil, and strive with Thy help to be of assistance to all men.

And lead us not into temptation, hidden or manifest, sudden or protracted.

And deliver us from evil, past, present, and future.
So be it, with good will and without hope of reward.

Francis of Assisi (1182-1226) is an Italian monk, saint, and founder of the Franciscan order based on the vows of poverty, chastity, and obedience.

2. DANTE ALIGHIERI, *PURGATORIO XI*

Our Father in Heaven, not by Heaven bounded but
there indwelling for the greater love
Thou bearest Thy first works in the realm firstfounded,

hallowed be Thy name, hallowed Thy power by every
creature as its nature grants it
to praise Thy quickening breath in its brief hour.

Let us come to the sweet peace of Thy reign, for if it
come not we cannot ourselves
attain to it however much we strain.

And as Thine Angels kneeling at the throne offer their
wills to Thee, singing Hosannah,
so teach all men to offer up their own.

Give us this day Thy manna, Lord we pray, for if he
have it not, though man must strive
through these harsh wastes, his speed is his delay.

As we forgive our trespassers the ill we have endured,
do Thou forgive, not weighing
our merits, but the mercy of Thy will.

Our strength is as a reed bent to the ground: do not
Thou test us with the Adversary,
but deliver us from him who sets us round.

Dante Alighieri (1265-1321) is the greatest Italian poet. The Divine
Comedy *is his masterpiece.*

3. PHYLLIS TICKLE

Our Father, we—I and those, both seen and unseen, who join me in these words, and those others whom our love brings to this prayer by proxy—greet You as source, essence, and totality of life; and in the union of familial concern, we beseech Your all-powerful mercy upon us and all whom You have created.

Who art in Heaven, the One Who is in an Is-ness which we do not know and can not imagine, but which we suspect, in our moments of transport and meditation, of being everywhere and all-where beyond the capsule of our dimensions, of being the surrounding place of Light that defines our darkness, of being the final purpose that explains us.

Hallowed be Thy Name, which wraps the unnameable core into whose depths we fall when in prayer and with which our bereft and wretched consciousness always and everywhere seeks consummation.

Thy kingdom come both here and hereafter, both now and forever, which words we offer in petition both for our souls' sake and as an oath of fealty to Your Beauty.

Thy will be done on earth as it is in Heaven; for there are worlds of influence and affairs so much larger than both my small life and our many lives that we will die, Father, unless there are some safe havens for our spirits here on earth, some hostels of peace and pockets of obedience to restore and encourage us. And beyond that, Father, we have loved the world Your will has created; and we ask You, of Your great mercy, to redeem it both in Your Son and through our lives that it may grow before You into the creature of Your intention.

Give us this day our daily bread and grant us freedom from the faithless destruction of asking for more. Make us agents as well of sustenance for all those who, in whatever words, raise this same petition to You.

Forgive us our trespasses as we forgive those who trespass against us; for Your grace only can free us from the hell within time of the condemnation of each other, of rancor, and of resentment. Be merciful, Father, and free us from this most corrupting and corrosive curse of our kind. Cause us as well to see— but shield us from despair in our looking—our own hideous sins, lest we closet them out of sight and unconfessed in fear of one another.

Lead us not into temptation whether perceived or hidden, for only through Your gracious help can we escape it or, having fallen, be allowed to survive it. Keep us instead, beloved Father, constantly in passionate love with the harmony of Your Law, constantly seduced by the mystery of Your Word.

And deliver us from evil, both material and spiritual, that our lives, as well as our words, may praise You and we may come to rest at last within Your holy Name when Time is ended.

Phyllis Tickle is a writer on prayer and religion. Among her many books are The Divine Hours *and* The Shaping of a Life.

4. BISHOP SERAPHIM SIGRIST

Our Father, Abba, and first of all letters, *who art in heaven,* the Omega to the Alpha of the one we meet as *abba* with infinite trust at the first point of knowing ourselves as separate,

Hallowed Kiddush! sanctified by every offering we make opening our hands and hearts, *be thy name* the name whose letters fill the sky.

Thy kingdom which is that Name, which is the joining of all letters in a music beyond Mozart or Pythagoras, *come* as it is always coming both remote and near with a speed without limit.

Thy will be done, and it is even I who must both receive, "be it unto me according to thy word" and also act it, for "I am come to do thy will O Lord,"

On earth always grounded, in the dark and warm where fire is at the foot of the mountain imaging Grace, *as it is in heaven* for our little light, lit by Grace tended by action and love, reflects the lights above.

Give us this day our daily bread The Day is the bread you give us, as the manna faded from moment to moment, a day of it gone in a day, the Bread is the day is the bread, just this moment you give us "containing in itself all sweetness,"

And forgive us our trespasses, the bread discarded, the letters unread or unwritten, letters falling like leaves, the word of joined lives we have not made,

As we forgive those who trespass against us and in so doing make the word, receive the bread, work again with the letters joining them as fallen leaves to the Tree of Life now a Splendor of Forgiveness,

And lead us not into temptation may we not stray into crooked ways or ever come to the place where we have forgotten our name and so also yours,

But deliver us from evil in saying your name Risen One!, *Om* . . . Abba! the Victory, from Kingdom, . . . in power unafraid to act though we live to be a hundred, to the Glory, *le Olam,* To the Ages, *Eis Aioni* . . . we are Thine. Amen.

Bishop Seraphim Joseph Sigrist is an Orthodox writer and teacher. His books include The Rainbow Sermon *and* Theology of Wonder.

5. LAUREN WINNER

Our Father—We pray as a collective. We come to You as Your Body. For centuries, Hebrew benedictions were uttered by the People of Israel only as *we,* and I would not know how to begin to approach You now were it not for my community, the church, teaching me how to pray and praying alongside me. And yet we pray to a Father who loves us, not merely as a plural, but as individual children. You are the God who numbers the hairs on our heads. You are the God who knows our needs before we can pronounce them. We petition in plural, and You know us in our blessed singularity.

Who Art in Heaven—Father, sometimes I eavesdrop on my own prayer. When I listen to myself pray, I hear that I usually whisper this phrase into one breath, as though it were only a statement of Your geography, of Your residence: You live in heaven. But it is also a statement of Your being. Yes, Your being happens up there, out there, over there in heaven, but that is perhaps secondary to the fact that You are. Our Father, Who Art. Our Father-God, Who Is.

Hallowed be Thy Name—Father God, You, whose name is holy, whether or not we stop to sanctify it. Not only You, but we are hallowed in the making of this prayer. *To hallow* is not merely *to make sacred*, but also *to make ready*. And to pray this prayer is a kind of ready-making. We make ourselves ready for the kind of contemplation that can follow spoken prayer. We make ourselves ready for a day of cross-bearing and kingdom-proclaiming, by reminding ourselves who and what we are, and who and how our Father is.

Thy—Here is where the contemporary language can help: Yours. We ask that Yours be done. Everything that is Yours. Not our broken, fallible, misguided desires and designs, but Yours Yours Yours. Your will, Your power, Your vision, Your love, Your order. And we ask that we, too, will come to belong to You. That You seal us in Your love, that You shelter us with Your wings. Everything that is Yours, everything that is Thy, be done.

Kingdom Come—With this alliterative urging, we point ourselves toward a sort of Advent apocalypticism. We ask not only for You to come as a squalling baby in a manger, or as a gentle friend and shepherd and companion on the way, but as a King, as a victor who will destroy evil and reign triumphant. Here our adjectives for You, God, are not only gentle, but also sovereign. Here our images are not just staffs, but also scepters. Here we become monarchists, pleading that Your kingdom come.

Thy Will Be Done On Earth, as It is in heaven—To borrow from St. Teresa of Avila, "The pay begins in this life." This is a statement of the most basic faith. That You have a will, a vision, a wish for Your Creation; and that Your will is perfect, that it is better than anything we could ask or imagine. And, still more daring, that the doing of Your will is not remote, pie-in-the-sky, but here on our homely and humble earth, here, the kingdom of God.

Give us this day our daily bread—My small, navy blue Book of Common Prayer directs me to say the Lord's Prayer at many intervals in the day, including, in the service of compline, very late at night. It is hard to know what to think of the petition for daily bread at the end of a long day in which I have been blessed with plenty of bread, not to mention cheddar cheese, yogurt, pesto sauce, carrots, and wine. And so, at the end of the day, I offer this petition as a plea for circumspection in spending and eating; that You will bless me not with bounty, but with moderation; that You will grant me daily bread, but only just. This is thanks that I have always had enough, and a petition that in the coming days and weeks I will have enough, but not too much.

And forgive us our trespasses as we forgive those who trespass against us—This is the rub, forgiving those who hurt us. We're not offering a back-room bargain: "God won't forgive your sins unless you forgive your neighbor's." Forgiveness is rather a process. Your forgiving us inclines us to forgive. And forgiving my neighbor—who may have stolen my horse, or cut me with an insult, or kept me waiting at a coffee shop for forty-five minutes, or maybe my neighbor is someone dearer, a parent who failed me or a spouse who cheated on me, or a friend who betrayed me—forgiving her saves my prayer from woo-woo spirituality, and presents prayer as a practical tool for my daily routine, for the sanctifying of ordinary life.

Lead us not into temptation—The only temptation our culture pays much attention to is the lure of food—of rich chocolate, of ice cream, of strawberry smoothies and crunchy Oreos and Toblerone bars. Our magazines and talk-show hosts offer tips for warding off the temptation of that extra piece of pie, and tips for hiding the evidence of our indulgence when we give in. But temptation is not principally about snacking. It is principally about sin. And temptation seems ubiquitous: we are tempted when we drive past shopping malls, we are tempted by the charming flirt in our office, we are tempted to adultery and gossip and idolatry and despair. Thus, this straightforward petition. That You will guard us from the devil, and from the desires of our own hearts. We can ask this because Jesus is incarnate; we can ask because Jesus was tempted in the desert. Yet this is not merely a petition. It is also a statement of self-knowledge. We know ourselves to be *creatures*. We know how little we can take. So we ask not that You will give us steel-wills when temptation comes, but that You will prevent us from ever even edging near temptation. We ask that You will lead us somewhere better, somewhere more upright, somewhere truer, and, yes, somewhere easier. Because we know how we slip and slide and stumble. We know our righteousness is not a matter of our will, but of Your provision.

But deliver us from evil—An unquestioned assumption: that evil exists. That power and principalities play poker for our souls. That we live estranged from You and from each other, fallen. But there is not one corner of this fallen world that You do not claim. There is no home or tree or conversation that You are not redeeming. This coda is less a petition than a statement of things as they are. It is the You, the God we name as Father, the God who forgives, and whose name is Hallowed, who delivers us from evil. *Amen.* So be it.

Lauren Winner is the author of Girl Meets God *and* Mudhouse Sabbath. *She lives in Charlottesville, Virginia.*

6. CHRISTOPHER BAMFORD

Our. You are the Father of us all. You exclude no one. You know us all. You know that when we pray our prayer is not a personal petition. We put ourselves aside. As You are universal, our prayer is universal. The universe prays in and with us. When we say "our," we mean everyone, all beings, not only human beings. The angels in heaven, the dead, all creatures on earth—all plants, insects, birds, and animals—all times and places, mountains, rocks, rivers, and oceans—everyone joins with us in this prayer. When we say "our" the entire creation and all that is in it prays with us, for we all come from You and return to You. We are all Your creatures. We only return to You what is Yours. But this solidarity with all creation is no vast generality. It is a delicate intimacy and love. We love You. We pray to You. By this "You," You give us all.

Father, Abba. Loving source and origin, primal goodness and existence, giver of all and every gift, You come before all. You are first. Hidden, in secret, You call and we respond. You are our true north. You loved us first. Through Your love, You allow us to find ourselves, orient ourselves, and know where we are. You created us for this: to be known in us. We return the gift You gave us. We call You "Father." You are the Father of Your Son, by whom we are all sons and daughters and heirs.

Who art. You ARE beyond "are"—infinite, groundless consciousness—beyond being itself.

In heaven. No visible, locatable place, below or above, to the left or the right, distinguishable from other places, but rather the place of all places, all heavens and all earths. Invisible then, and without location, universal, outside space and time, infinite and eternal. Not only nowhere, but nothing.

Hallowed be. You alone are holy, pure, perfect, whole, firm, without any partiality and separateness. Therefore, all the angels sing, "Holy, Holy, Holy."

Thy. By this little word "Your," we are. "You" come first. By this You, we become. You create us. You call us into being. Turning toward You, addressing You, are the consciousness and love we are.

Name. Your name describes the activity by which You are and are known. You are present in Your name. You are Your name. You are Father, but You are also Son, and Spirit. Your name is Goodness, Word, Beauty. You are Creation, Incarnation, and Redemption. You are existence, intelligence, desire. Your name is Loving, Merciful, Creator. Light of the World. You are Wisdom, too, for Your name is also Spirit. You who dwelt among us, died with us and for us, and rose again to be with us to the end of the world, have mercy on us. For You are all-merciful, and all-loving, and all-knowing.

Thy Kingdom come. Your Kingdom is the endless round-dance of the Trinity—the unity-in-difference of love's perpetual, sacrificing circulation. When Your Kingdom comes—when it is—every being will be in its place in perfect peace. May that day come. We await it in joyous, hope-filled trembling.

Thy will be done. Your desire is to be all in all, to be known and loved in all things. For this You became human: that we too might become divine like You, and participate in Your knowing, being, and loving. Sadly, we confess our desire is not always Your desire, or will—Your way is not always our way. Help us discern Your will.

On Earth as it is in heaven. In heaven, the angels adore You, chanting "Holy, Holy, Holy."

Give us. Father, You give us everything. You give us Your Son and Your Spirit. You give us the world and all that is in it. You give us our life, our senses, our hearts and minds. Whatever we are You have given us.

This day our daily bread. Without Your divine sustenance, Your grace daily received, we could not live at all. Freely, You sustain us from moment to moment. Our gratitude knows no bounds.

Forgive us. To forgive is to let go—what we do not hold onto is no longer. More than that, to forgive is to give. It is a gift—the greatest gift and blessing. You let go of all that in ignorance and opposition we interpose between us. You give us Your love, which is our being— the love that first loved us and created us and sustains us, which we are and return to You.

Our trespasses. Every day we crucify You by our turnings away and forgettings, our silent blasphemies, betrayals, and denials. Forgive us all the ways we place obstacles to Your presence, abusing Your love that surrounds us and flows through us from Your creatures and meets us in everyone we meet, and love, and work with. May we be one in You.

As we forgive them that trespass against us. Help us to let go of all these obstacles as You let go of them, to give as You give, and to love as You love—impartially, universally, and personally. Each day, help us to wipe the mirror clean and meet each other as new born in Your love; help us turn to each other over and over again in love and friendship, seeing in every face, in every eye, always Your face, our original face.

Lead us not into temptation. The temptation is not to see You, not to behold Your face, but to see only ourselves, our own countenances—to take, not give, to close off and defend, not open and receive. When we lead ourselves, we lead ourselves into egotism. Therefore, we ask You to lead us away from ourselves toward You.

Deliver us from evil. This is evil—that we arrogate all power to ourselves, that we think and feel and act as if You did not exist. That we forget You and seek to fulfill only our own needs and desires. Father deliver us from the egotism and selfishness that puts us out of harmony with Your own perfect timing and deludes us into believing we can create the world in *our* image.

Amen. I believe.

Christopher Bamford works in publishing and is the author of Voice of the Eagle *and* An Endless Trace: The Passionate Pursuit of Wisdom in the West.

The Lord's Prayer in Movement

The following series of movements of the body are based on ancient Christian prayer postures. Each phrase of the prayer is accompanied by a particular posture. From an attitude of containment, the postures move upward, downward, and outward, returning again to one of containment, completing a circle.

These postures may be taken standing, or sitting on a cushion or a chair. Move through them several times, learning the postures thoroughly before praying within them.

Maintain an awareness of the whole body in each posture and be especially attentive as you follow the movement between one posture and the next.

Arrive at a posture and allow the phrase of the prayer associated with it to arise. Speak it aloud, and sense the vibration of the sound as it resonates. Remain in the posture for the space of a breath or two before continuing. Prepare before moving, and accompany the movement to the next posture with a sensed awareness of the body.

Begin by gathering your attention in stillness and quiet for a few moments.

1   Hands straight down if standing, or resting on thighs if seated, head straight.

2 ## Our Father
who art in heaven

Arms fold over chest, right arm over left, fingers touching shoulders, as head bows down.

3 Hallowed be Thy name

Moving together, head comes up as elbows lift. When elbows arrive slightly above shoulder level, the lower arms unfold, palms outward.

4 Thy kingdom come

Head remains up, palms rotate toward each other and elbows lower to shoulder height as arms open slightly wider than shoulder width and palms relax upward (as though holding a large ball). Fingers are diagonally forward.

5 Thy will be done

Head bows down.

6 On earth as it is in heaven

Arms come down to rest on thighs if seated, straight down if standing, as head comes up to straight.

7 Give us this day our daily bread

Upper arms against body lightly, elbows at right angles, palms up, fingers slightly relaxed.

8

And forgive us our debts as we also have forgiven our debtors

Arms straight out to the side, palms down.

9

And lead us not into temptation

Palms turn upward and elbows release slightly as head bows.

10 But deliver us from evil

Arms fold over chest, right arm over left, fingers touching shoulders. (posture 2).

11 Amen

Hands come straight down if standing, or down to rest on thighs if seated, as head comes up to straight.

Remain a few moments when the sequence ends, sensing the breathing and the body as a whole. Dwell alertly within the atmosphere of the prayer. Recognize when your attention begins to weaken, and intentionally finish your period of prayer before becoming lost in daydreaming.

Allow the body to be relaxed and open during the sequence. Be especially attentive to the shoulders, making sure they remain down and do not become hunched and tense as the arms raise or extend.

If you wish, repeat the prayer sequence a second time.

Acknowledgments
and Sources

To my editor, Lil Copan and publisher, Lillian Miao, my gratitude. To the contributors who accepted the invitation to share their encounter with the prayer, my abiding fellowship. To Sister Pat Young of the Leo House in New York, and to Karyn Chao, Caroline Herrick, and Eugene Romanosky, whose reading of and response to the manuscript was invaluable, my deepest appreciation.

Ayo, Nicholas. *The Lord's Prayer: A Survey Literary and Theological.* Lanham, MD: Rowman & Littlefield, 1992.

Becker, Karl, and Marie Peter, comps. and eds. *Our Father: A Handbook for Meditation.* Translated by Ruth Mary Bethell. Chicago: Henry Regnery, 1956.

Bonhoeffer, Dietrich. *Meditating on the Word.* Edited and translated by David McI. Gracie. Cambridge, MA: Cowley, 1986.

Brock, Sebastian, trans. *The Syriac Fathers on Prayer and the Spiritual Life.* Kalamazoo, MI: Cistercian, 1987.

Cassian, John. *John Cassian: The Conferences.* Translated and edited by Boniface Ramsey. New York: Paulist, 1997.

Chariton, Igumen of Valamo, comp. *The Art of Prayer: An Orthodox Anthology.* Translated by E. Kadloubovsky and E. M. Palmer; edited by Timothy Ware. London: Faber and Faber, 1966.

Congar, Yves. *I Believe in the Holy Spirit*. Translated by David Smith. New York: Seabury; London: G. Chapman, 1983.

Dante Alighieri. Excerpts from *Purgatorio* from the *Divine Comedy*. Translated by Luca Ciardi. Copyright 1954, 1957, 1959, 1960, 1961, 1965, 1967, 1970 by the Ciardi Family Publishing Trust. Used by permission of W.W. Norton & Company, Inc.

Ebeling, Gerhard. *The Lord's Prayer*. Translated by James W. Leitch. Brewster, MA: Paraclete, 2000.

Evdokimov, Paul. *Ages of the Spiritual Life*. Original translation by Sister Gertrude; revised translation by Michael Plekon and Alexis Vinogradov. Crestwood, NY: St. Vladimir's Seminary Press, 1998.

Evely, Louis. *We Dare to Say "Our Father."* Translated by James Langdale. New York: Herder and Herder, 1965.

Flavel, John. *On Keeping the Heart*. An abridgment is available from Christian Classics Ethereal Library, at http://www.ccel.org/f/ flavel/keeping/keeping.html.

Fosdick, Harry Emerson. *The Meaning of Prayer*. Folcroft, PA: Folcroft Library Editions, 1976.

Francis of Assisi. *St. Francis of Assisi: The Legends and Lauds*. Edited, selected, and annotated by Otto Karrer, translated by N. Wydenbruck. New York: Sheed & Ward, 1952.

Gregory of Nyssa. *The Lords Prayer and The Beatitudes*. Translated by Hilda C. Graef. Westminster, MD: Newman, 1954.

Guardini, Romano. *The Lord's Prayer*. Translated by Isabel McHugh. Manchester, NH: Sophia Institute, 1996.

Hopkins, Gerard Manley. *Poems and Prose of Gerard Manley Hopkins*. Edited by W. H. Gardner. London: Penguin Books, 1953.

Hopko, Thomas. *The Lenten Spring: Readings for Great Lent*. Crestwood, NY: St. Vladimir's Seminary Press, 1983.

Hügel, Baron Friedrich von. *Letters from Baron Friedrich von Hügel to a Niece*. Edited by Gwendolen Green. London and Toronto: J. M. Dent & Sons, 1929.

Hugh of Balma and Guigo de Ponte. *Carthusian Spirituality: The Writings of Hugh of Balma and Guigo de Ponte*. Translated by Dennis D. Martin; preface by John Van Engen. New York: Paulist, 1997.

Ignatius of Loyola. *The Spiritual Exercises of St. Ignatius of Loyola*. Translated by Elder Mullan. New York: P. J. Kennedy & Sons, 1914.

Jeremias, Joachim. *Abba: the Prayers of Jesus*. Translated by John Bowden and Christoph Burchard. Philadelphia: Fortress, 1978.

——— *The Lord's Prayer*. Translated by John Reumann. Philadelphia: Fortress, 1964.

Johnston, William, ed. *The Cloud of Unknowing and The Book of Privy Counseling*. New York: Random House, 1973.

Kadloubovsky, F., and G. E. H. Palmer, comps. and trans. *Early Fathers from the Philokalia*. London: Faber and Faber, 1954.

Kadloubovsky, E., and G. E. H. Palmer, trans. *Unseen Warfare*. London: Faber and Faber, 1952.

Kelpius, Johannes. *A Method of Prayer*. Edited by E. Gordon Alderfer. New York: Harper Brothers, 1950.

Kovalesky, Eugraph. *A Method of Prayer*. Based on the third French edition by Esther Williams; edited to conform to the fifth French edition by Robin Amis and Raymond Hébert. Newburyport, MA: Praxis, 1993.

Law, William. *The Spirit of Prayer, or The Soul Rising out of the Vanity of Time, into the Riches of Eternity*. London, 1749. Available from Christian Classics Ethereal Library at http://www.ccel.org/l/law/prayer/.

Lochman, Jan Milic. *The Lord's Prayer*. Translated by Geoffrey W. Bromiley. Grand Rapids, MI: William B. Eerdmans, 1990.

Louf, André. *Teach Us to Pray*. Cambridge, MA: Cowley, 1992.

Luke, Helen M. *The Voice Within: Love and Virtue in the Age of the Spirit*. New York: Crossroad, 1987.

Luther, Martin. *The Large Catechism*. Translated by F. Bente and W. H. T. Dau. Triglot Concordia: The Symbolical Books of the Evangelical Lutheran Church. St. Louis: Concordia Publishing House, 1921. Also available at http://www.lcms.org/president /aboutlcms/bookofconcord/largecatechism.asp.

MacDonald, George. *Unspoken Sermons*, Third Series. Eureka, CA: Sunrise Books, 1966.

——*Creation in Christ*. Edited by Rolland Hein. Wheaton, IL: Harold Shaw, 1976.

A Manual of Eastern Orthodox Prayers. Crestwood, NY: St. Vladimir's Seminary Press, 1999.

Merton, Thomas. *Dialogues with Silence: Prayers and Drawings*. Edited by Jonathan Montaldo. San Francisco: HarperSanFrancisco, 2001.

——*New Seeds of Contemplation*. New York: New Directions, 1961.

Moran, James. "Image and Likeness: An Interview with Bishop Kallistos Ware." *Parabola: Myth and the Quest for Meaning* Vol.10, no.1 (1985): pp. 62–71.

O'Connor, Flannery. *A Good Man Is Hard to Find and Other Stories*. New York: Harcourt, Brace, 1955.

The Philokalia, volume 2. Translated and edited by G. E. H. Palmer, Philip Sherrard, and Kallistos Ware. London and Boston: Faber and Faber, 1981.

Powell, Robert, trans. *Meditations on the Tarot: A Journey into Christian Hermeticism*. New York: Jeremy P. Tarcher, 2002.

Rolle, Richard of Hampole. Cited in *Spiritual Direction and Meditation,* by Thomas Merton. Collegeville, MN: Liturgical Press, 1960: p. 84.

Schmemann, Alexander. *Our Father*. Translated by Alexis Vinogradov. Crestwood, NY: St. Vladimir's Seminary Press, 2002.

Schürmann, Heinz. *Praying with Christ: The "Our Father" for Today*. New York: Herder and Herder, 1964.

Speyr, Adrienne von. *The World of Prayer*. Translated by Graham Harrison. San Francisco: Ignatius, 1985.

Tauler, Johannes. *The Inner Way*. Edited by Arthur Wollaston. London: Methuen, 1902. Also available from Christian Classics Ethereal Library at http://www.ccel.org/t/tauler/inner_way/inner_way.htm.

Teilhard de Chardin, Pierre. *The Divine Milieu: An Essay on the Interior Life*. New York: Harper & Row, 1960.

Teresa of Avila. *The Way of Perfection*, in *The Complete Works of Saint Teresa of Jesus*. Translated and edited by E. Allison Peers from the critical edition of P. Silverio de Santa Teresa. London: Sheed & Ward, 1946.

Weil, Simone. *Waiting for God*. Translated by Emma Craufurd. New York: G. P. Putnam's Sons, 1951.

The Wound of Love: A Carthusian Miscellany. Kalamazoo, MI: Cistercian Publications; London: Darton, Longman & Todd, 1994.